Cover image used courtesy of the Minnesota Historical Society.

Hexagon Star | Date: c. 1885 | Maker: Mrs. H. D. Morse
Size: 60" x 72" | Owner: Stevens County Historical Society

Minnesota Quilts

Creating Connections with Our Past

PHOTOGRAPHY BY Greg Winter & Lee Sandberg

TEXT BY the Minnesota Quilt Project

FOREWORD BY Helen Kelley

Voyageur Press

Edited by Kari Cornell
Designed by Julie Vermeer
Printed in China

05   06   07   08   09   5   4   3   2   1

Library of Congress Cataloging-in-Publication Data:
Minnesota quilts : creating connections with our past / text by
the Minnesota Quilt Project ; photography by Greg Winter and
Lee Sandberg.
     p. cm.
Includes bibliographical references and index.
ISBN 0-89658-079-2 (hardcover)
1. Appliqué--Minnesota. 2. Patchwork quilts--Minnesota. 3.
Quilting. I. Minnesota Quilt Project.
TT779.M58 2005
746.46'09776--dc22
                2004025524

Distributed in Canada by Raincoast Books
9050 Shaughnessy Street
Vancouver, B.C. V6P 6E5

Published by Voyageur Press, Inc.
123 North Second Street, P.O. Box 338
Stillwater, MN 55082 U.S.A.
651-430-2210, fax 651-430-2211
books@voyageurpress.com
www.voyageurpress.com

*Educators, fundraisers, premium and gift buyers, publicists,
and marketing managers:* Looking for creative products and
new sales ideas? Voyageur Press books are available at special dis-
counts when purchased in quantities, and special editions can be
created to your specifications. For details contact the marketing
department at 800-888-9653.

About the Quilt on the Cover and Fron-
tispiece: The quilt on the cover was made by Elizabeth Waller. Elizabeth was born near London, England
(date unknown), and died in 1896. It is not known
when she came to the United States, but she lived
most of her life in and around Chicago, Illinois. She
had friends in Minnesota whom she occasionally visited, and it is assumed that on one of those visits, most
likely in February 1887, she saw the St. Paul Winter
Carnival Ice Palace.

The center of that palace was an octagonal-
shaped tower, measuring 135 feet tall. The ice palace
on Elizabeth's quilt also appears to be octagonal, and
it is surrounded by arches and turrets that resemble
those in pictures of the 1887 palace. Family stories indicate that Elizabeth started this Crazy quilt in 1887
and finished it five years later. The ice palace on the
quilt is surrounded by twenty blocks, which contain
various designs. Blocks pieced in "Crazy" work form
a border around the twenty blocks, and a wide velvet
border edged in silk ball fringe frames the outer edge.

Elizabeth's Crazy quilt contains intricate embroidery
and appliqué work, much of which is three-dimensional and embellished with beads and other orna-
mentation. The fabrics include silks, satins, velvets,
and even discarded kidskin gloves, which she made
into a cluster of grapes. Some of the motifs that Elizabeth used—spider and spider web, a lyre, an anchor,
and a fan—are often associated with Crazy quilts.
One unusual block features the White House, set in
the quilt on the diagonal. Elizabeth's family was posi-
tive that she had never been to Washington, D.C., but
there was an encyclopedia in her home that contained
an early picture of the White House. It closely resem-
bles Elizabeth's rendition, so she may have used the
picture for reference.

Elizabeth's granddaughter, Marguerite Kennedy,
donated the quilt to the Minnesota Historical Society
in 1959. Marguerite remembered when "we children
had a chance to have it spread out and enjoyed . . . I
used to look at it as a child and wonder how such a
quiet old lady could think up such beautiful things."

Acknowledgments

The Minnesota Quilt project wishes to acknowledge that this book exists because of the efforts of hundreds of volunteers throughout the state of Minnesota who organized Quilt Discovery Days; urged their friends to bring quilts to be documented; created records for the quilts discovered; hung, photographed, and folded quilts; secured locations; and prepared treats and food for volunteers. Although we can't name each and every one of the nine hundred volunteers, their efforts contributed to the success of the project and this book.

We wish to acknowledge the following people for their extraordinary efforts with the project: JoAnn Braun, Avis Lageson, Dorothy Stish, and Jeanne Spears, who hosted the first organizing meeting in 1986 which precipitated this project. Norm Steere, Kathë Lemmerman, Jean Hatch, and Allene Helgeson, who worked tirelessly on organizing the Quilt Discovery Days. Helen Kelley, who generously donated her time and expertise on dating quilts. Sr. Mary Lou Murray, CSJ, and Judy Sears, who organized the oral history project in conjunction with the Quilt Discovery Days. Generous financial grants from the Minnesota State Historical Society and Minnesota Quilters enabled this project to begin. Gifts from local guilds allowed us to continue the documentation process. We also wish to express our thanks and appreciation to the owners of the quilts featured in the book who allowed us to collect and transport their family treasures to Minneapolis to be photographed for the publication. Our photographers, Greg Winter and Lee Sandborn, used their skill with lenses, cameras, and lighting to complete the stories of these quilts with beautiful images. Their response to the quilts and the stories about the quilts made the photography sessions a learning experience for all involved. We wish to thank our able editor, Kari Cornell of Voyageur Press, who smoothed and polished our words as well as blending our chapters into a whole. And, of course, we wish to thank our families for their patience as we neglected them to meet deadlines even as they served to bolster our confidence in our ability to complete this project.

**Mexican Rose | DATE: c. 1850
MAKER: Unknown; made as
wedding dowry for Lucy Anne
Kingsley Nash | SIZE: 76" x 87"
OWNER: Sibley House, Minnesota
Historical Society**

Dedication

This book is dedicated to the Minnesota quiltmakers who shared their knowledge, creativity, ideas, and friendship with the generations of quilters who came after them; to those who have treasured the quilts, including family, friends, collectors, and historians; and to today's quiltmakers, who continue the legacy for the next generation of quilters.

Chinese Puzzle | Date: **c. 1890s** | Maker: **Kate Wise** | Size: **77" x 77"**
Owner: **Stevens County Historical Society**

Contents

Foreword

BY HELEN KELLEY

Minnesota is a large and vibrant state. When I first came here from the East Coast early in the 1960s, I was impressed with the energetic newness of the area. There was a forthright, frontier quality about it that is still evident even in the large cities. For instance, as an East Coast native I was taught never to discuss money, religion, or politics. My neighbors here post signs in their yards, advertising their political choices. This is part of that free and vigorous quality. I admired that openness when I first came, and I still do, now. This fresh approach is especially evident among the quilters here. They have an enthusiasm, an eagerness, and a generosity that makes being among them and working with them a pleasure.

This is a state of contrasts. Geographically, the landscape in Minnesota ranges from the Mississippi River bluffs on the eastern border to the great grassy prairie land on the western edge, and to the north, there are lakes surrounded by woods so dense that some areas are still only accessible by canoe. Culturally, the extremes range from contemporary sophistication and pride in a fine educational and artistic scene to the peace of remote farmlands.

The people are a study in contrast too. The state has a large Native American population and an astonishing mix of immigrants who have come to call this area their home. Though this territory has in the past been thought of as a "Little Germany" or "New Scandinavia," a very diverse group of people, including those of African, East Asian, and Middle Eastern descent, call themselves Minnesotans today. They have come to this promised land as refugees, students, and skilled workers. These are the people who make up an eclectic and exciting community.

All of this has a bearing on the current state of quilting in Minnesota. One hundred and seventy-five years ago, the first missionaries packed their suitcases and came up the Mississippi River on boats to bring "civilization" to the "Indians." They settled in the woods along the rivers and lakes. In addition to introducing Christianity and the European way of life to the Native peoples, the missionary women from the East Coast taught the Native American woman how to quilt. The missionary intent was to teach them a "gentle art" and to encourage them to abandon their itinerant lifestyle and become a stable, European-style farming population. Early on, the Native American women used their quilting skills to raise funds for their mission church activities. Then, as the buffalo disappeared across the plains, quilts became bed and body coverings that replaced the vanishing buffalo robes. In the 1900s quilts took on another significant role for Native Americans; they endowed star quilts with a spiritual significance, and these quilts became honor gifts, a symbol of gratitude. Thus, those first quilts, which were made according to that traditional American style, have become a significant contemporary cultural expression.

This same kind of change has happened across the board with Minnesota quilts. Our early American quilts consisted of appliquéd or patchwork blocks made of standard geometric shapes. The early settlers used quilts for bedding and for protection from the elements. Over the years, in that traditional format, quilts have been made to raise money, to be given to families in crises, to create communal bonds among family members, and, in the hard times, to provide pleasure in a difficult world by creating beautiful things with soft textiles. Today's quilter is a sophisticate. She can make traditional quilts if she longs for the structure of tradition or she can create quilts that are arty and exotic, spun from the fibers of her own mind.

Now, as new cultures interact with the old, established ways, an exciting thing is happening to our quilts. Many of the newest-comers to the state have brought their own needlework traditions with them. These arts, the contemporary and the traditional, are crossing paths. I have seen amazing hand-appliquéd fabrics of the Hmong women of Laos and Thailand quilted into bed coverings by Amish women. I have seen Javanese batiks pieced into contemporary friendship quilts. The spontaneous designs of rural African-American quilts have inspired "art quilters" to work within a less restrictive format. With changing demographics and more varied textile resources, "The Minnesota Quilt" is being redefined even at this moment. As a Minnesotan and as a quilter, I owe a debt of gratitude to the cadre of historians from the Minnesota Quilt Project, who have traveled this state for the better part of two decades. They have photographed and documented quilts that had been hidden away in at-tics, folded up on closet shelves, stowed in basement boxes, or consigned to car trunks for emergency use. These quilts have been cherished through the years. Many of them are tattered or faded now. This corps of documenters has carefully and reverently captured the history of these quilts and their makers.

This book includes pictures of several of those quilts. Some of the traditional quilts were carried to this state in pioneer trunks. Others were created here to keep the settlers warm through the biting cold of Minnesota winters. Here in this book the team of quilt history researchers have captured our past, and that is significant.

Thank you to all the quilt owners who have shared their treasures with this project. Thank you to all of the quilt researchers, drivers, photographers, and equipment handlers who played an important part in documenting each quilt. And thanks to each of you who have supported and encouraged this endeavor. You have created an important document.

Introduction

BY JEAN LOKEN

Our mothers, grandmothers, and great-grandmothers worked very hard during their long and productive lives, but most of the products of that toil were either eaten, outgrown, or just got dirty again. If they made quilts, however, those quilts were often saved and cherished, lasting long after their makers were gone. In 1987, the Minnesota Quilt Project (MQP) was formed to try to locate and document the history of these quilts and the women and men who made them. We hope that by studying these quilts—the fabrics, patterns, sizes, and the way in which the quilts were given and used, we might better understand the lives of our ancestors here in Minnesota.

Minnesota Quilters, Inc. (MQ), the statewide quilt guild in the North Star State, was formed in 1978 and now has 1,300 members in the United States and Canada. Some of its members are also active in the American Quilt Study Group, where they learned about the growing popularity of state quilt documentation projects. Under the auspices of MQ, those with an interest in quilt history called for volunteers to organize a Minnesota quilt documentation project.

In a series of Quilt Discovery Days (QDD), quilt owners brought quilts to designated sites throughout the state to recall memories of their foremothers as more than nine hundred volunteers recorded the information. We chose QDD sites based on the availability of local sponsors and coordinators, which were usually guilds or county historical societies. In the first three years, we held thirty-nine QDDs throughout

Red on white appliqué quilt top | DATE: c. 1880 | MAKER: Margaret Wilson | OWNER: Otter Tail County Historical Museum

The maker's daughter and recipient of the top, Mrs. Cecil W. (Jessie) Sherin, was a prominent member of the Pelican Rapids community. She was a graduate of Queens University in Kingston, Ontario, and she succeeded her husband as president of a bank in 1956, a position she held until her death in 1973. She was active in the Red Cross during both World Wars. Although it was never quilted, this striking paper-cut style appliqué top is in good condition. The family donated the quilt to the Otter Tail County Historical Museum in 1975.

Quilt Discovery Day Locations

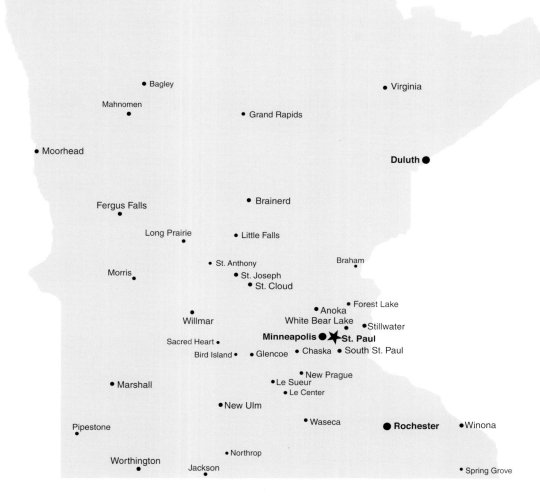

the state and documented two private collections. In 1997, we added two sites in Minneapolis and St. Paul to document quilts in the African-American community and began the search for county museum and private collections. In another phase of the project, we searched the documentation from our QDDs to locate quiltmakers who would make interesting subjects for oral history interviews, and we sent volunteers out to tape their stories.

We will continue to document quilts in the state during new QDDs, and we encourage those with quilts made before 1976 and with some connection to Minnesota to contact the project. We also urge quilt owners to document their own quilts to keep the history alive for new generations.

Although the training manual for volunteers who were at the reception area of QDDs advised them to accept quilts with some connection to Minnesota and quilts made before 1976, this was not strictly enforced. Because of the relatively late settlement of the state, we realized that people might bring in many fine quilts that were not made in Minnesota. We were amazed to discover in one of our small state museums located on the banks of the Minnesota River just across from Fort Snelling, the first fort established in the state in 1820, a quilt made before that date, perhaps in the last quarter of the eighteenth century. And we were charmed to document a quilt made in 1974, picturing a family home in a Crazy quilt style.

The Minnesota Quilt Project received major grants from MQ and the Minnesota Historical Society and gifts from small guilds to fund our research. We offered to the public memberships in the project and were pleased to receive an excellent response. In 1997, we cooperated with both the Minnesota Historical Society and the Minneapolis Institute of Arts to mount exhibits of representative quilts. In 1999, we mounted our own exhibit in South St. Paul with almost one hundred quilts.

In the early days of the MQP, two members visited the Otter Tail County Historical Society in Minnesota to photograph a few quilts and learn more about the documentation process. One quilt they saw, a red on white appliqué quilt top made by Margaret Wilson, so affected them that it became the logo of the project.

The MPQ board arranged training sessions for volunteers. We were fortunate to have Helen Kelley for quilt dating, Katy Christopherson for documenting, and later, Jeanette Lasansky for oral history. The textile curators for the Minnesota Historical Society, especially Marcia Anderson, were on hand to offer advice.

In the original group of forty-one QDDs, there are 3,337 quilts. Of those, 828 quilts were made in the 1930s, and 400 quilts were made in each of the decades before and after the 1930s. Forty-five quilts were made before the Civil War. The makers of 185 quilts chose to sew or pen a date on theirs. The earliest dated quilts—a set from Duluth including a baby quilt and a large presentation quilt—were inscribed with 1844. Both were made in Philadelphia and are featured in chapter 3. We were pleased that 126 quilts, including twenty-four Crazy quilts, were both signed and dated.

The most popular pattern among the documented quilts was the Star, in all its variations, with 381 total.

This beautiful quilt, once displayed at the former DAR museum, remained in the same family for seven generations. One of its owners was a descendent of William Brewster, who arrived on the Mayflower.

Candlewick quilt, whole cloth cotton | Date: **c. 1776** | Maker: **Jane Shaw**
Size: **92" x 97"** | Owner: **Sibley House Museum collection**

Linda is a fiber artist who quilts and makes character dolls. She writes, "The house on 'Harvest Quilt' was built by my great-grandfather in 1900 and has been home to five generations of my father's family. My brother and sister-in-law live there still. The sunset design was inspired by my mother's mother and her use of neckties to make quilt blocks in a fan design. My quiet Gramma survived the Great Depression with dignity and humor and her necktie quilts were just one example of her thrifty artistry. I was 20 in 1973 when I had this idea for my own necktie quilt sans neckties. Although neckties were nowhere to be found, fabric shops were abloom with the psychedelic colors and flower prints of the hippie era. This quilt represents for me, a childhood securely rooted in our big old house and the bright warmth of a creative family in the hopeful idealistic 60s."

Harvest quilt | DATE: **1974** | MAKER: **Linda Cogelow** | SIZE: **68" x 79"**
OWNER: **Private collection**

Crazy quilts were the second most popular, with 378. Considering the relatively short period in which Crazy quilts were made, the large number of quilts documented speaks volumes for their popularity. It's possible, too, that Crazy quilts were more likely to be preserved, because they were used as bedding less often than other quilts were. The third most popular pattern was Grandmother's Flower Garden with 228. Other popular Depression patterns, Dresden Plate, Double Wedding Ring, and Baskets, also made top ten list of recorded patterns. The perennial favorite, Log Cabin, came in fourth place.

Only about half of the documented quilts had known makers, and about 12 percent of the makers were born outside of the United States. Of course many of these quilters arrived in Minnesota as children, but one may see this as an indication of the rapid assimilation of Minnesota's immigrant population. Women were exposed to the culture of their neighbors in church, at the market, and in community groups, and interviewees named all of these places for learning to quilt. Only 2 percent of the makers were unmarried, and 15 percent had attended college or university. Al-

most 30 percent had only completed grade school and 35 percent were farmers. The professions of many of the quiltmakers show the wide variety of activities open to women in towns and cities in the late nineteenth and early twentieth centuries. There were 184 teachers, 30 nurses, 22 telephone operators, 45 bakers or cooks, 35 secretaries, 11 milliners, 12 postal workers, 8 midwives, and 18 business owners, mostly of cafes, boarding houses, and shops. The MQP also documented eight male quiltmakers, one of whom was said to be a prolific quilter during his retirement years.

But some of the most colorful remembrances of the makers are the personal comments of their children, nieces, and others, which appear throughout the book. Janet Medalen of Duluth, the granddaughter of Catherine H. Peterson Reamer, recalled that "Grandma belonged to a quilt club, but she wouldn't let them work on her quilts."[1] Arlene Millard of Rosemount inherited a quilt made by her grandmother, Isabell McDonald Smith, born in Scotland. Arlene's mother then paid someone in Creighton, Nebraska, to quilt the top in 1924 and was charged by the spool. When she saw the bill she said that she "didn't need to quilt it so much."[2]

Necktie | DATE: late 1960s | MAKER: Gena Eleanor Loken Fretham | SIZE: 51" x 69" | OWNER: On loan to the Houston County Historical Society

Gena, the oldest of ten children, was born October 13, 1901. She learned to quilt at an early age and is unsure how many quilts she has made. She used a treadle machine until her family's home got electricity at the end of World War II, when she got an electric machine. She started a quilt as soon as she finished one. In creating this necktie quilt, Gena challenged herself to make use of discarded neckties. She feather stitched around each piece before backing and binding the quilt. The piece is unquilted.

The writers of the following chapters illustrate how quilts connect us to the times in which they were made, to the family and community events for which they were created, and to the popular culture that influenced their designs. Even if the exact history of the quilt is unknown, it can be placed in the context of our history based on its fabric, size, or pattern. Quilts continue to speak to us across time, connecting us to our ancestors. For this reason, quilts have become a resource for historians, especially those who study women's history. Political and social trends are also apparent in quilts. We will continue to use quilts and enjoy the comfort they provide, while remembering the value they will hold for anyone studying the lives of our predecessors. Minnesota has a rich quilting history that we have only begun to explore.

Wheel | Date: c. 1890–1910 | Maker: Unknown
Size: 69" x 89" | Owner: Beverly Tesch

The owner purchased this colorful quilt through an antique dealer in southern Minnesota. The quilt is enhanced with a virtual encyclopedia of embroidery stitches in crewel thread. A border of wedges and large scallops in red wool frame the quilt. It is backed with cotton sateen. The utilitarian fabrics of wool and rayon come alive in this quilt. The maker also included silk and velvet, harkening back to the height of the crazy quilt era.

Chapter One

Connections to Minnesota History

BY LAURA JELINEK AND ELISE SCHEBLER ROBERTS

The history of Minnesota unfolds through the stories of quilts and quiltmakers. For more than one hundred and fifty years, Minnesota women and men have sewn together fabric scraps and added filler and backing to create quilts filled with warmth and love. Representing many nations and traditions, successes and failures, hopes and fears, Minnesota quiltmakers shared their skills with family, community, and the world. You don't have to be a quilter to feel the power of quilts. They draw you in, evoking memories of family and friends. Whether you are a quiltmaker or quilt lover, this chapter's quilts and stories will take you on an exciting tour of Minnesota history.

Early History

Minnesota is a land of geographic diversity—evergreen forests to the north, deciduous woodlands along the rivers, grasslands in the west, and hills and marshes to the south. Now called "the Land of 10,000 Lakes," the state actually boasts more than 14,000 lakes, remnants of glaciers that covered the area only ten thousand years ago. Minnesota is home to the headwaters of the continent's greatest river, the Mississippi, which begins its 2,350-mile journey at Lake Itasca in Clearwater County. Over the centuries, diverse groups of people have called Minnesota home.

While Europeans were just beginning to explore the eastern part of North America, the Dakota had lived in the land they called "Mi-ni-ma-ko-ce" for many generations. They lived a migratory life, moving throughout the land with the changing seasons. In the winter they hunted moose, deer, elk, and buffalo. In the spring they tapped maple trees to make sugar. All summer they tended their cornfields and gathered berries and herbs, and in the fall they harvested wild rice.

Eastern tribes, pressured by European settlement, moved west into the land of the Dakota. The Ojibway, also known as Chippewa or, in their native language,

Anishnabe, relocated to the area around Lake Superior. For many years the Dakota and Chippewa were bitter enemies. The other name for the Dakota, "Sioux," is part of the Chippewa word for "enemy."

The French encountered these two tribes as they explored Minnesota in the late 1600s. Since the enmity between the two tribes made travel and trading difficult, the French, led by Daniel Du Luth, pushed them to negotiate a peace. In the early 1880s, Father Louis Hennepin and Pierre LeSeur explored the upper Mississippi seeking new trade routes. Soon French traders, also known as voyageurs, regularly crossed the lands of the Dakota and Ojibway, trading European-made items for animal pelts, especially beaver.

Once European explorers "discovered" Minnesota and introduced their way of life to the Native Americans, the lives of the Dakota changed dramatically. The Dakota, who had never had horses before, divided into two groups—those who moved to the western plains to ride horses and hunt buffalo, and those who remained in their established villages and fields, developing new trade networks with the French and competing with the Ojibway for animal pelts. Old disagreements were re-ignited, and soon the Dakota and Ojibway were again enemies. With the availability of trade goods from the Europeans, both tribes reduced their production of many household and agricultural tools. The trade relationships between the voyageurs and the native peoples lasted nearly one hundred fifty years.

The Arrival of the Europeans

By 1800, several countries, including France, England, Spain, and the United States of America, maintained a claim in the Minnesota territory. It was the Louisiana Purchase, signed in 1803, that placed the entire region under the control of the United States. Two years later Lieutenant Zebulon Pike held a meeting with the

Dakota at the junction of the Mississippi and Minnesota Rivers to try to negotiate for a piece of land on which to establish a fort. He was successful, but the War of 1812 and other national events delayed construction of the fort for fourteen years.

The United States government finally built Fort Snelling in 1819. Colonel Josiah Snelling, who moved to Minnesota with his wife and family from New England in 1820, supervised the construction. Soldiers serving at the fort had a responsibility to protect United States fur traders from the English traders in Canada and to maintain peaceful relationships with and among the Dakota and Ojibway. The American Fur Company trading post and the Indian agency were both near the fort, in present-day Mendota. Within a few years, the families of soldiers and traders had also moved to Minnesota.

By 1823, steamboats were able to navigate the Mississippi to St. Anthony Falls in present-day downtown Minneapolis, making it easier for more settlers to come to the area from the eastern United States. The growing demand for more space was the impetus for the first of many treaties that ceded Dakota and Ojibway lands to the United States in 1837. Vast tracts of uncut forests attracted the lumber and sawmilling industry, which offered jobs to anyone willing to move to the area. People of English, Irish, and Scottish descent came from New England, New York, Pennsylvania, and Canada to work in the lumber industry. Farmers would later settle the land that was no longer of value to the lumber companies.

The promise of jobs and land brought more families to new territories. Women brought quilts with them or made quilts on the way, often replicating and transforming quilt patterns to reflect their new lives. These quilts not only kept travelers warm along the way but also became part of the families' new homes. Some completed quilts were carried in dowry trunks; others arrived in pieces to be completed at a later date in a new location hundreds of miles from their origin. Still other quilts that traveled west were gifts to those making the journey, and these treasured objects found homes where their makers had never been. Quilts brought a sense of history to their new locations, made the new dwelling home, and served as protection against the cold. A few quilts traveled across the better part of North America to be with the descendants of their makers, providing visual connections from east to west, from north to south, and from the past into the future.

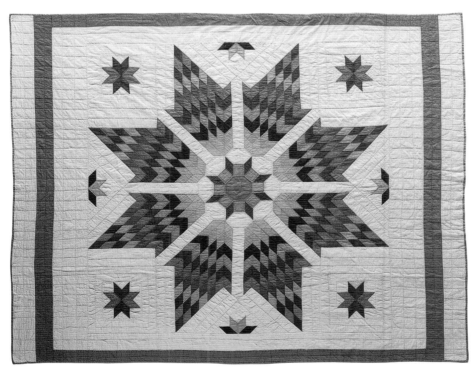

Star Quilt | Date: c.1910 | Makers: Indian Women's Sewing Circle | Size: 66" x 84" Owner: Liz Beran

This quilt was made by Yankton Sioux Women between 1900–1910. It was a wedding present for Winnifred and Guy Barton. The quilt was handed down through the family to its current owner, Liz Beran.

SUNBURST QUILTS

Pieced and quilted by the family of Nancy Cormany for her dowry, this Sunburst quilt was made around 1830. Nancy, who was born in 1815, married John Pomeroy White in 1839. The couple moved from Annsville in Lebannon County, Pennsylvania, to Mount Carroll County, Illinois, shortly after their marriage. They carried all their household belongings in a covered wagon, including a large, heavy wooden trunk filled with quilts. After Nancy died in 1894, the quilt remained in Illinois until about 1905, when it

was given to a family member, who brought it to her seaside cottage on Long Island in New York. It eventually returned to Illinois. The quilt traveled to Minnesota in the late 1930s, where it has remained along with the wooden trunk brought by covered wagon to Illinois so long ago.

The quilting includes feathered wreath, tulip, and daisy shapes. The batting is of raw cotton, with seeds still intact. The colors of the quilt were originally blue and red before fading to a green and pink. The bind-

Sunburst | DATE: c. 1830 | MAKER: unknown | SIZE: 72" x 82" | OWNER: Phoebe Sells

This Sunburst quilt made for the dowry of Nancy Cormany.

Sunburst | Date: 1848 | Maker: Mary Jane Barnhart Root | Size: 73" x 92" | Owner: Elsie Mooers

Mary Jane pieced this Sunburst quilt when she was fourteen years old.

Left: Mary Jane Barnhart Root, circa 1919.

ing has been replaced twice. The quilt could have been made with the help of Nancy's Pennsylvania Dutch relatives or her in-laws who came from Scotch or English tradition, as the Sunburst pattern is known to both.

When Mary Jane Barnhart Root, born in 1834, migrated from Mooers Fork, New York, in 1850, pieces of this Sunburst quilt moved with her. Pieced when she was just fourteen, the quilt and its maker traveled from upstate New York to the Minnesota territory, eventually settling north of Fort Ripley. The quilt remained unfinished while Mary Jane homesteaded, raised nine children, and became a healer with knowledge of roots, herbs, and medicine. Neighbors often called upon her when the doctor was unavailable. She charged nothing or worked for trade.

Mary Jane's father was a sea captain, and the Sunburst pattern of this quilt is similar to the Mariner's Compass pattern, symbolizing her transformation from a mariner in New England to pioneer on the Minnesota prairie. In 1937, eleven years after Mary Jane's death, her granddaughter, Alise Mooers Foster, completed the quilt.

Detail of autograph

Album quilt with central medallion | DATE: **c. 1848** | MAKER: **Unknown**
SIZE: **87" x 90"** | OWNER: **Collection of Sibley House Historic Site**

This Autograph Cross wedding quilt was made for John and Nancy Aiton.

ALBUM QUILT WITH CENTRAL MEDALLION

In the mid 1800s, most Dakota villages along the St. Peter and Mississippi Rivers had a Christian mission school created by the Boston-based American Board of Commissioners for Foreign Missions (ABCFM). From the point of view of the missionaries, it was not an easy decision to accept an assignment in "Indian Territory." Writing from her parent's home in Quincy, Illinois, a romantic, naïve Nancy Hunter encouraged her betrothed in a letter dated February 16, 1848: "How could Providence speak more plainly than to us [;] it seems to speak 'Labor for the Indian.' Their souls are precious & soon the opportunity to labor for them ceases forever." Her fiancé, the somewhat more realistic Rev. John Aiton, wrote from his Cincinnati Seminary, "I have been Anxiously revolving our going to the Sioux, in my mind . . . My own physical courage is very small."

In the end, the couple decided to join the mission project. Prior to departing for their ABCFM assignment, Nancy and Aiton married in Quincy in July 1848, when Nancy was twenty-three years old. This handsewn Album quilt with appliqué medallion was a wedding gift from family and friends at the Mission Institute of Theopolis. Each of the sixty-one handpieced blocks has fine handwriting and careful ink signatures. These passages wish the couple not only well in their marriage but also in their impending assignment to Redwing mission. "Go ye therefore to / teach all nations/ Lo I am with you always. / Matt/ 28:19, 30."

By mid August, the couple's modest belongings, including this quilt, were ensconced within the elm-bark village at Red Wing, where the Many Rattle-snakes Band of Dakota lived. There is no doubt that the Aitons faced difficulties and the cultural alienations associated with life on the prairie. After less than three years at the school with her husband, Nancy Hunter Aiton died of pulmonary consumption in 1854.[1]

On the Way to Statehood

By 1848, the settlement populations had expanded to the point that a group of men, headed by the American Fur Company's Henry Sibley, requested that Minnesota become a legal territory of the United States. The United States government established Minnesota as a territory in 1849, and Alexander Ramsey, a Pennsylvanian, was appointed as the first territorial governor. St. Paul became the territorial capital.

Migration and immigration to Minnesota continued through the 1850s. Settlers from New England, the Mid-Atlantic states, and the eastern Midwest were joined by immigrants from Ireland escaping famine, Germans seeking political freedom and Swedes and Norwegians fleeing religious persecution. Immigrants named their new towns St. Patrick, Scandia, and New Ulm in recognition of their origins.

CARPENTER'S WHEEL QUILT

The Tindall family moved from the eastern United States to Shelbyville, Indiana. This Carpenter's Wheel or Double Star quilt was one of six or more quilts made by Lydia A. Tindall, who was born in 1832. The quilt is dated 1850 and was most likely used on the Tindall's farm. Lydia's granddaughter, Edith Jones Woodward, a graduate student of astronomy at Harvard University, took the quilt back east. After Lydia died in 1903, her great granddaughter-in-law, Judy Woodward, rediscovered the quilt on a family member's bed. Paul Woodward, Judy's husband and Lydia's great-grandson, took the quilt to California and then to Minnesota in the 1980s, where it remains a treasured heirloom.

The Carpenter's Wheel is associated with a wagon wheel or farm life; the block symbolizes movement, which aptly describes this quilt's journey.

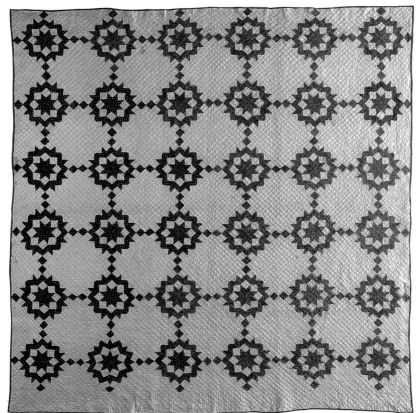

Above: Lydia Tindall of Shelbyville, Indiana

Carpenter's Wheel | DATE: 1850 MAKER: Lydia Tindall | SIZE: 76" x 79" | OWNERS: Paul and Judy Woodward

Carpenter's Wheel quilt, signed and dated 1850

Tree of Paradise | **Date:** 1857 | **Maker:** **Julie Coon**
Size: 71" x 72" | **Owner:** **donated by Warren Kirsch**
to the Aitken Historical Society

Tree of Paradise quilt made by seamstress Julie Coon

Tree of Paradise Quilt

Seamstress Julie Coon made this Tree of Paradise quilt in 1857. Born in Connecticut in 1824, she brought the quilt with her when her family moved to Vernon Center, Minnesota, in the 1890s to establish a farm. Julie made approximately fifty quilts before she died in 1928.

Bold red trees against the white background left ample room for Julie to show off her quality quilting, including seven to eight stitches per inch in rows quilted one inch apart. Quilters in the last half of the nineteenth century favored figurative designs such as trees, houses, and baskets, pieced into blocks.

Quilts were made to comfort the afflicted, raise money for charitable causes, celebrate rites of passage, and commemorate historical events. This appliqué sampler, known as the "Charlotte Burns Quilt" after the largest name embroidered on the quilt, provides a historical record of the world around its makers. Little is known about the quilt or its makers, but the Masonic symbols and the seven embroidered names of women who lived in Stillwater imply that the quilt may have been made for the Stillwater Masonic Lodge in 1859.

Minnesota Statehood & the Civil War

In the early 1800s, immigrants arriving on the East Coast quickly made their way to the heart of the country, thanks to improved transportation on the waterways and the expansion of the new railroad system. In a very short time, the Minnesota Territory had many farms and growing towns. It became the thirty-second state in 1858 and was soon involved in the Civil War, fought in the East and South.

When the Confederate Army fired upon the Union at Fort Sumter, South Carolina, in April 1861, Minnesota became the first state to offer troops to the Union cause. Although only 150,000 people lived in the Minnesota Territory before the war began, by the end of the Civil War more than 25,000 Minnesotans had served. Since Minnesota was a free state, very few of these men had experience with slaves or slavery. They were, nevertheless, anxious to serve their new country.

With their husbands, fathers, and brothers gone, women found themselves responsible for maintaining businesses and farms in addition to child rearing, sewing, cooking, and tending to the household. For many women, these were long years, characterized by loneliness, worry, and financial burden.

Appliqué sampler | DATE: 1859 | MAKERS: Unknown SIZE: 76" x 78" | OWNER: Warden House, Washington County Historical Society

This appliqué and embroidered quilt made for a four poster bed includes the names of seven women who lived in Stillwater, Minnesota, in 1859.

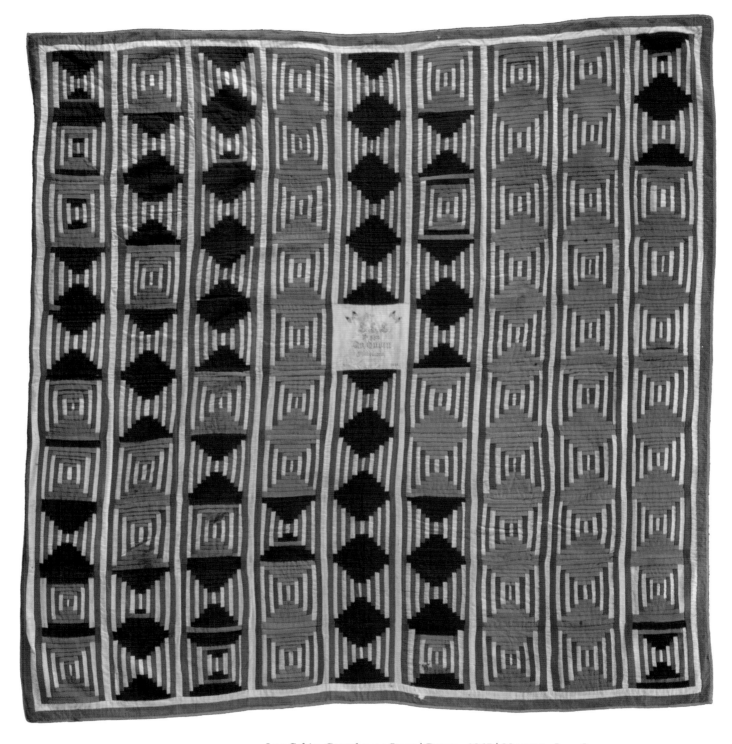

Log Cabin, Courthouse Steps | Date: **1865** | Maker: **Lucy Lamson**
Size: **79" x 80"** | Owner: **Collection of the Minnesota Historical Society**

Civil War quilt made from wool and cotton (Courtesy of Minnesota Historical Society)

Red and green appliqué sampler quilt | DATE: **c. 1865** | MAKER: **Unknown** | SIZE: **72" x 80"** | OWNER: **Helen Quist**

Heavily quilted green and red appliqué quilt, circa 1865

LOG CABIN, COURTHOUSE STEPS QUILT

Lucy Lamson of Homer, Minnesota, was born in 1820 and died in 1888. She made this Log Cabin Quilt in 1865 for her son. A soldier for the Seventh Minnesota Regiment Company B, he was fighting in Mississippi for the North. The embroidered quilt is made of red, white, and blue wool foundation pieced on various cottons including ginghams and plaids. The center inscription reads "L.L.L. No. 352 DuQuion, Illinois May 1865." L.L.L are presumably the quiltmaker's initials, but the rest of the inscription remains a mystery.

During the Civil War, many quilts were made in response to the "sanitary fairs" that were established to provide for the health of the army. The Sanitary Commission solicited donations of food, bedding, and medicine to supply the hastily established military hospitals. It is estimated that seven thousand lo-cal women's aid societies donated as many as twenty-five thousand quilts. Even though this quilt was probably not part of the commission's drive, its patriotic colors and red and white stripes make a bold political statement.

RED AND GREEN APPLIQUÉ SAMPLER QUILT

Little is known about this quilt's history. It was made in 1865 for Anna Deem Argetsinger by her aunt. The name of the quilter is not known, but she is reported to have been one of the first missionaries to cross the Appalachian Mountains. She used the red, green, and white palette common during this period but added less common accents of yellow. The quilt was expertly quilted at ten stitches per inch in rows quilted one-half inch apart.

The Dakota Conflict

Just one year into the Civil War, an event within the state's borders drew the attention of both government and citizens. In 1851, the Dakota tribe and the United States government had entered into the Traverse des Sioux and Mendota treaties. These treaties, made in good faith, opened Minnesota for increased white settlement and forced the Dakota onto a small portion of land along the Minnesota River. The Dakota were dependent on the little hunting they could do on their lands and the treaty payments from the U.S. government.

In the summer of 1862, the government was deeply involved in the Civil War and neglected to make treaty payments. The Dakota were starving, and a few, in desperation, attacked and killed a family of white setters. This event ignited a war, which lasted for several months and consumed much of western Minnesota. Many frightened white settlers took refuge at Fort Ridgely and at New Ulm, where fighting intensified. Finally Henry Sibley led a group of volun-teers from Fort Ridgely up the Minnesota River and contained the violence. As many as five hundred white settlers lost their lives, and thirty-eight Dakota were found guilty of murder and eventually hanged. The remaining Dakota were taken to camps in South Dakota, where many died of starvation and disease.

Although the Ojibway did not participate in the war, white settlers feared them as well and pushed the government to form the White Earth Reservation, where the Ojibway moved in 1868.

LOG CABIN DIAGONAL FURROWS QUILT

When Helen Williamson married Herbert Lyman at Greenwood, South Dakota, in 1912, she received this traditional Log Cabin Diagonal Furrows Quilt as a gift. Helen's father, John P. Williamson, was a well-known Minnesota missionary at the Redwood Mission Station, Lower Sioux Agency. He writes of the quilters, "One, and sometimes two quilts are quilted nearly every week in the year. The women take turns bringing

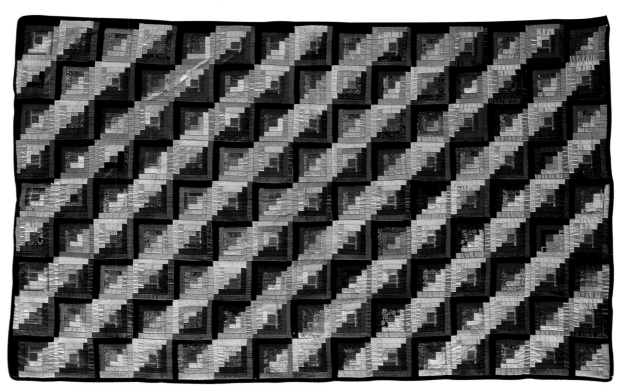

Log Cabin Diagonal Furrows | DATE: c. 1912 | MAKER: Indian Women's Sewing Circle | SIZE: 40" x 64" | OWNER: Ted Beran

This quilt was given to Helen Williamson when she married Herbert Lyman in Greenwood, South Dakota, in 1912

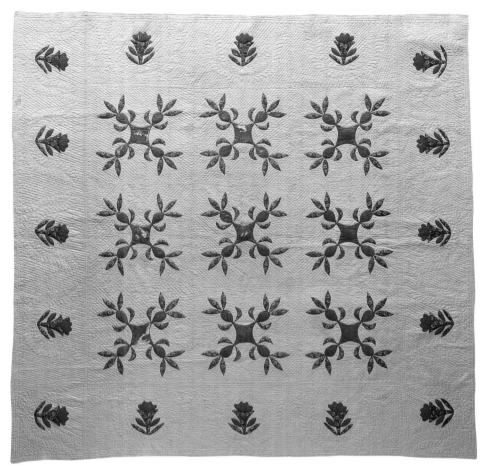

Red and green appliqué with Flowers and Buds | DATE: c. 1869 | MAKER: **Mary Elizabeth Hamilton Farrand** | SIZE: 84" x 84" | OWNER: **Robert Brown**

Red and green appliqué quilt with trapunto

and serving a noon lunch. One room contains a long table, a cook-stove and a cupboard of dishes."[2]

Williamson accepted voluntary exile at Fort Snelling, along with the Dakota people following the 1862 Dakota Conflict in southwestern Minnesota. Helen and Herbert moved to Lemmon, South Dakota, where their daughter Sara was born. Sara moved to Minnesota to teach in Sanborn and was surprised to discover she had moved to within forty miles of where her grandfather began his missionary work. She later married Ted Beran, and they lived on a farm near Clements. When Helen died, Sara inherited her quilts.

RED AND GREEN APPLIQUÉ WITH FLOWERS AND BUDS QUILT

Mary Elizabeth Hamilton Farrand, born in 1839, hand appliquéd this quilt in 1869. Mary was born in Vermont and came to Belle Prairie, Minnesota, in 1855 to join her sister Lucy Hamilton. Lucy helped found the Ayre Mission School in 1849 near Fort Ripley where she taught Ojibway children.[3] Lucy sent for family members, including her sister Mary.

Mary married in 1856. She completed this quilt on the day her daughter was born. Mary had nine children including two sets of twins. Mary died in 1901. The background contains many quilted patterns, including traditional feather patterns and crosshatching. The nine squares are traditional appliqué; Mary most likely designed the flowers appliquéd in the border. The appliqué designs are padded with homemade batting; the cottonseeds are visible.

Growth and Prosperity

Immediately following the Civil War, Minnesota was a center of rapid growth and new industry. The railroad connected Minneapolis and St. Paul to the rest of the United States by the 1870s, thanks to the work of James J. Hill. New towns sprung up almost overnight along the lines to serve both the farmers and the trains.

Along the Mississippi at St. Anthony Falls, grain mills joined the lumber mills. By 1880 Minneapolis produced more flour than any other city in the nation.[4] The mills spurred the growth of a related industry, the manufacture of flour and feed sacks, which would become an important component of many Minnesota quilts.

Sunburst | **DATE: 1872** | **MAKER: Francis Knight Ward** | **SIZE: 75" x 79"**
OWNER: Rosemary Ward Hill

Francis began quilting as a girl and made at least fifty quilts, including this Sunburst or Lone Star quilt.

Eight-Pointed Star
DATE: c. 1875
MAKER: Juliet
Phillips Gordon
SIZE: 98" x 102"
OWNER: Nancy
Ralston

Eight-pointed star quilt, made circa 1875

SUNBURST QUILT

Francis Knight Ward was born in Ravensville, Wisconsin, in 1857. She and her husband moved to Kansas City, Kansas, in the 1880s. This Sunburst quilt, most likely made in 1872, was one of more than fifty quilts Francis made. In 1924, her son, Madison Jacob Ward, moved to Proctor, Minnesota, to work for the railroad. Before she died in 1940, Francis gave Madison the quilt as a gift during one of his return visits to Kansas. He eventually passed it on to his daughter, Rosemary Ward Hill, who lives in Duluth.

EIGHT-POINTED STAR QUILT

Juliet Phillips Gordon, born in 1817, grew up in Laurenceville, Pennsylvania. As a young girl she traveled with her father, Dr. Joseph Phillips, through the Pennsylvania countryside. Dr. Phillips, who served in the army in the 1790s, showed his daughter sites of important battles and taught her early American history.

Later in life, Juliet reflected back on her father's sense of history in an interview with the *Duluth News Tribune.*

> *"I can remember the stories he used to tell us of his army service on the frontier and about being stationed in Detroit, which was the only town that had a hotel . . . Both Detroit and Pittsburg were frontier towns in those days."*[5]

In the article, Juliet was described as a grand old lady whose "spirit of friendship beams out from her dear old eyes."

She moved to Duluth in 1886 to live with her son, James Frederick Gordon. Her handpieced Eight-Pointed Star quilt is patriotic yet earthy in tone, in colors reminiscent of military uniforms. Juliet died in 1917 at the age of 100.

T Block or Cross Within a Cross variation | DATE: **1883**
MAKER: **Grandma Jones** | SIZE: **66" x 80"** | OWNER:
Edith Buhler

This quilt is signed "Grandma Jones" next to the year 1883.

The Industrial Revolution

In the late nineteenth century, new technology and scientific methods were introduced on the family farm. With the railroads, farmers could easily move their products to markets across the country. Increased demand led to a need for increased productivity. Farms became larger and more mechanized. In the western part of the state, large farms were harvested by itinerant crews of men and machines, who would work for several farmers over a period of weeks and move on. Minnesotan Oliver H. Kelly of Elk River and some friends organized the Patrons of Husbandry, commonly known as The Grange, to teach new farming methods. The Grange was the first major farm organization to accept both men and women as equal members.[6] Local Granges across the state also provided farm families with opportunities for social gatherings, including quilting bees, and political activism.

Major social movements were born in the nineteenth century. The United States celebrated its centennial in 1876. The Women's Christian Temperance Union (WCTU) gained momentum as its members battled the evils of liquor. Minnesota Civil War veterans joined the Grand Army of the Republic (GAR), which was dedicated to the support of Union Army Veterans. The first seeds of the Women's Suffrage Movement were also planted, and this movement grew rapidly throughout the state and across the country.

TEMPERANCE QUILT

In the nineteenth century, alcohol was cheap and alcoholism widespread. Many wives and mothers feared male alcoholism, which often resulted in abusive behavior, poor work habits, and use of family money to buy alcohol. The temperance movement empowered women, enabling them to implement social controls to improve their status. Through the WCTU, founded in 1874, women learned the art of public speaking and

became versed in political action, skills that would be crucial to women's suffrage. Membership peaked at more than 200,000 dues-paying members in the late nineteenth century.[7] As in all important women's movements, quilts reflected the struggles and triumphs and came to symbolize reform. The Drunkard's Path pattern was strongly associated with WCTU as were the blue and white colors. The WCTU members wore a white ribbon as a symbol of purity. The T quilt, such as this one by a woman known as Grandma Jones, was also popular, as *T* stood for temperance. Little is known about Grandma Jones.

CENTENNIAL ALBUM QUILT

Women celebrated the one-hundred-year anniversary of the country's founding in 1876 by creating patriotic quilts. This Christian Cross album quilt, made in 1876 by Sarah Flemming Barnes at the age of sixteen, is one such quilt. Sarah's family came from Springfield, Illinois, where her father served in the Civil War under the Illinois Militia. The family's home was reportedly near President Abraham Lincoln's home. The owner is Sarah's great-great-great-grandson. Sarah died in 1946.

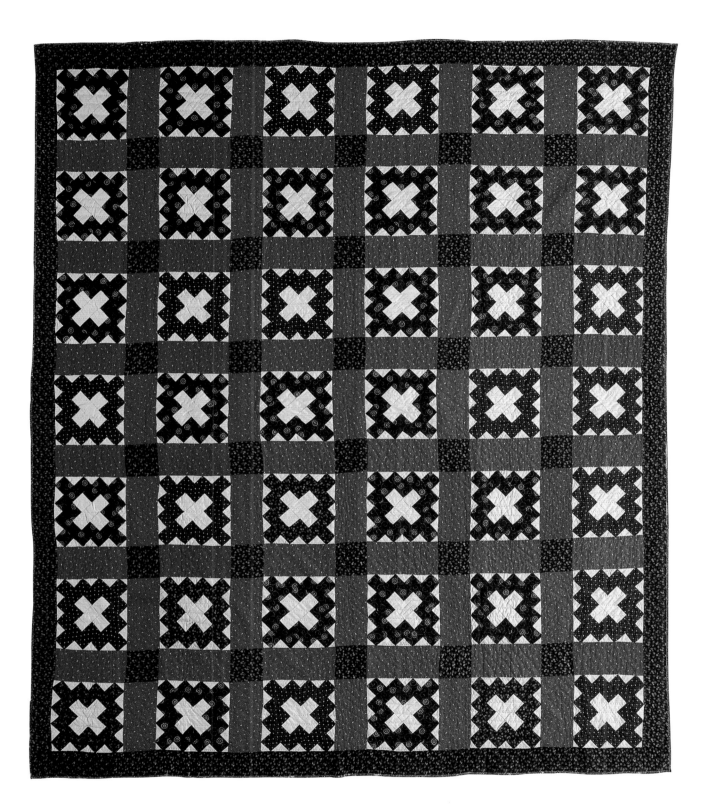

Christian Cross Album | DATE: 1876 | MAKER: **Sarah Flemming Barnes**
SIZE: 74" x 87" | OWNER: **Joe Butler**

*Handpieced patriotic centennial quilt
from 1876*

Scherenschnitte oak leaf | DATE: **1878** | MAKER: **Emma Engler** | SIZE: **73" x 89"** | OWNER: **Caroline Stark**

This appliquéd oak leaf quilt has the year "1878" quilted in the lower center.

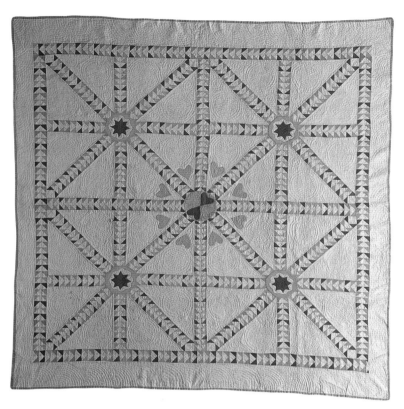

Flying Geese with stars and hearts
DATE: **1880** | MAKER: **Catherine Regan Sullivan** | SIZE: **72" x 72"**
OWNER: **Kathleen Minkler**

Catherine Regan Sullivan made this quilt when she was eighteen years old.

SCHERENSCHNITTE OAK LEAF QUILT

Emma Engler, who was born in about 1858, lived in various homes in Carver and Scott Counties. Emma was deaf and in the late nineteenth century she would have been considered "nonmarriageable" because of her disability. Like many women in her position, Emma became the family "domestic," living with whichever family member needed household help at the time. Emma often cared for her brothers' children, moving from house to house. She also did all of the family's sewing. The year "1878" is stitched in the lower center of this hand-appliquéd quilt. Emma lived to be more than one-hundred years old.

The quilt's owner is Emma's great-niece. The red and white color scheme peaked in popularity in the latter part of the nineteenth century. The sawtooth border was popular at that time and was often stitched in red and white.

Economic Changes in the Late 1800s

The latter part of the nineteenth century saw an increase in economic diversity. While some people made a lot of money in new industry and large-scale farming, a significant number of people, particu-larly new immigrants, lived in great poverty. Many immigrant women worked long hours in domestic or factory jobs and then came home to care for their families. The 1890s were characterized by alternating economic growth and financial recessions, called "panics." Fortunes were made and lost. Some of the greatest houses in the state, such as the James J. Hill House in St. Paul, were built with these fortunes.

FLYING GEESE QUILT

Catherine Regan Sullivan, who was born in 1862, made this quilt when she was eighteen. Catherine and her husband farmed in St. Thomas, Minnesota, and raised seven children. Catherine passed away in 1943, but the forty-acre farm is still in the family and farmed by Catherine's great-grandson.

Catherine, like many quilters, had no trouble mixing objects when creating designs. Stars, hearts, and flying geese are all represented in a single quilt. Although she did not sign the quilt, Catherine stitched a signature "K" in the red stars for her nickname, "Kate." The owner is a quilter just like her grandmother and great-grandmother Catherine.

COXCOMB QUILT

Mary Eleanor Simons Giddings most likely made this quilt after she arrived in Anoka, Minnesota, in 1854. Born on her family's farm in Williamsfield, Ohio, in 1833, she was the youngest of a large family of brothers. She and her husband, Dr. Aurora Giddings, traveled to Anoka by raft up the Mississippi River. At the time, Aurora was the only practicing medical doctor in the area north of Anoka to the Canadian border. He made regular trips to St. Cloud and Mille Lacs in his horse and buggy, under the cover of a buffalo robe.

Mary was active in the Methodist Episcopal Church, belonged to the Good Templars, and later became prominent in the Women's Christian Temper-

ance movement. Throughout her life, she continued to take classes at Chautauqua. Mary died in 1914.

Mary quilted in a crosshatch pattern around the appliqué. The border has trapunto work, done by carefully inserting extra padding after the quilting is finished.

Cultural Diversity

Immigrants from Russia, Poland, Romania, Czechoslovakia, and other Eastern European countries continued to settle in Minnesota in the early twentieth century. Many were Jews escaping the persecution

Mary Simons Giddings (second from left, middle row) in Anoka, Minnesota, circa 1910

Coxcomb Appliqué | DATE: unknown | MAKER: Mary Simons Giddings | SIZE: 80" x 83" | OWNER: Mary Jablonski

Appliquéd coxcomb pattern with raised-work border

Above: Quiltmaker Anna Sorn Sahr

**Original appliqué | Date: c. 1884
Maker: Anna Sorn Sahr | Size:
66" x 92" | Owner: Marilyn
Ekstrand**

*Anna made this quilt when she was
just sixteen years old.*

in Russia and nearby countries. A small number of Chinese immigrants also came to Minnesota. Unlike nineteenth-century immigrants who sought farmland, the new immigrants settled in cities and many opened their own businesses.[8] St. Paul and Minneapolis grew at a rapid rate, as young men and women left the state's farms and African Americans moved to northern cities from the South, all seeking economic and educational opportunities.

Original Appliqué Quilt

Anna Sorn Sahr was an avid quilter. Born in 1868, Anna moved with her parents in a covered wagon from Dundee, Illinois, to Minnesota when she was only two. The family discovered this quilt, which had not been used for years, among the belongings of Anna's daughter when she died in 1961. A note attached to the quilt stated that Anna had made it in 1884, when she was sixteen. Anna died in 1953.

Bold red and white stripes frame the appliquéd flowers set on point. A flying geese border surrounds both. The color scheme of this quilt—red, white, and green—was popular in the late 1800s. The green fabric in this quilt has faded. Anna likely created this pattern herself or adopted it from an existing pattern shared by friends and neighbors.

Original Design | Dᴀᴛᴇ: **1887**
Mᴀᴋᴇʀ: **Sarah Ann Bemis Gates**
Sɪᴢᴇ: **83" x 89"** | Oᴡɴᴇʀ: **Donald Crane Page**

Wedding quilt with embroidered date 1887, made by Sarah

Pieced Arrow
DATE: **1889**
MAKER:
**Lavina Gould
Smith** | SIZE:
76" x 83"
OWNER: **Helen
Hill Blanz**

*Pieced Arrow
quilt with
scalloped
borders, made
by Lavina*

WEDDING QUILT

Sarah Ann Bemis Gates, born in 1822, made this quilt as a wedding gift for her youngest daughter Ida. Sarah is a direct descendant of Miles Standish of the Plymouth colony in Massachusetts, and she and her husband raised four children in Vermont and Minnesota. Sarah died in 1913. The pattern is probably an original. The blue and white colors were as popular in the mid 1800s as they are today. Embroidered in the center is "Mrs. John Page," Sarah's daughter's married name, and "1887," the year of her marriage.

PIECED ARROW QUILT

Lavina Gould Smith made this Pieced Arrow quilt in 1889 at the age of twenty. The Smith family moved from Hamilton, Ontario, to Ohio; Lavina's husband was a minister, and the family moved around the state because of his job. After Lavina died in 1932, the quilt was passed down to Helen Smith Blanz (the owner's mother-in-law), who was a teacher in Moundsview, Minnesota. She gave the quilt to the current owner, Helen Hill Blanz, who recently retired to Colorado. Helen reports that Lavina was an avid quilter. She also received many quilts—most of them friendship quilts—believed to have been made by the women in the congregations her husband served. The scalloped edges are quilted with a swag design. Feather and clamshell designs are quilted in the plain blocks by an experienced quilter at nine stitches per inch.

Red Cross | DATE: **1919**
MAKERS: **Unknown** | SIZE:
66" x 83" | OWNER: **Stevens**
County Historical Society

This fundraising quilt has 145
hand-embroidered signatures.

Changes at Home and Abroad

While the United States was involved in World War I for only two years, more than one hundred twenty-six thousand Minnesotans served. Communities held fundraisers for the Red Cross. The men and women serving in Europe, many of whom had lived their entire lives in the United States, were introduced to both the terrors of war and the excitement of travel.

When they returned, the country was involved in a frantic economic and social evolution. Good economic times in the 1920s and the availability of new forms of entertainment, including radio, movies, and the automobile, fueled a renaissance in American culture, and Minnesotans gladly participated. Radio and movies provided people with in-

formation from around the world. The availability of the automobile not only increased mobility within communities but also gave rise to an entirely new industry—tourism. It was now affordable for the middle class to travel the country in ways previously only available to the wealthy. People could now live in one community and drive to work in another. The related agricultural-implement industry revolutionized farming, making it possible for farmers to manage larger farms, ultimately feeding more people.

RED CROSS QUILT

This quilt, made just after World War I in 1919, is typical of Red Cross fundraising quilts, with its bold red crosses and signatures. The organization raised money by charging ten cents per signature. Presumably, the large center signatures with stars were larger contributors. While this quilt's history is uncertain, it is believed to have been made by the Red Cross of Auxiliary School District 23 (the Messner school) of Hodges Township. A brief article in the February 28, 1919, issue of the *Hancock Record* reports that the school had a basket social, where single women would prepare picnic baskets to be auctioned to single men. The highest bidder shared the lunch with the young woman who made it, and the money went to charity. This Red Cross quilt was auctioned at the event for $39.

Basket and Vines | DATE: **c. 1900**
MAKER: **Virginia Gertrude Scoville Everhard** | SIZE: **76" x 83"**
OWNER: **Winifred Harris**

Virginia made this blue and white Basket and Vines quilt around 1900. It is machine pieced and machine quilted; the border is hand appliquéd. Virginia was born in Conneautville, Pennsylvania. She married John Jacob Everhard, a doctor, and moved to Kansas, then Minnesota, and eventually New York. The owner is Virginia's great-granddaughter.

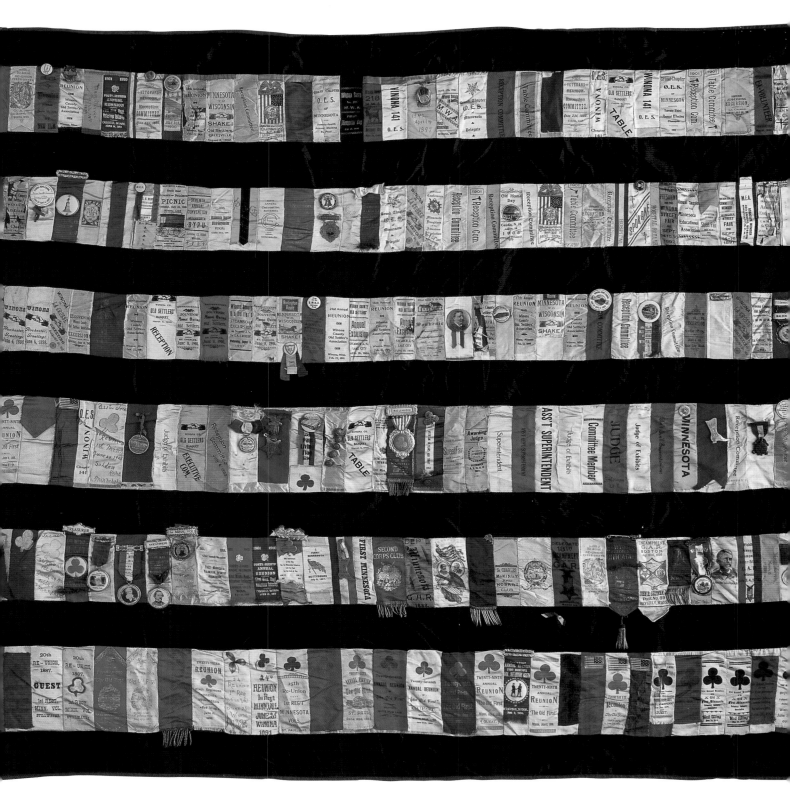

Ribbon | **DATE: 1925–1930** | **MAKER: Rose Bender** | **SIZE: 64" x 69"**
OWNER: Winona County Historical Society

Ribbon quilt made in the late 1920s
with ribbons dating from 1885 to 1925

Ribbon Quilt

Ribbon quilts such as this one, made by Rose Bender around 1925, seek to celebrate moments in history by using actual souvenirs as the building blocks. This quilt includes a wide variety of souvenirs, from ribbons from the Grand Army of the Republic (an organization of Union Civil War Veterans) to a Herbert Hoover lapel pin. It also celebrates Rose's personal history by including memorabilia from reunions and church functions. Rose, who was born in 1860, died in 1938.

The Great Depression

The stock market crash of 1929 brought prosperity to an abrupt halt. The Great Depression of the 1930s was a defining time for Minnesotans. Unemployment was high, work days were long, and wages were low. Men,

either alone or with their families, traveled the state and country seeking new jobs. Women did whatever job they could find—laundry, agricultural work, and waiting tables. Many people lost their homes, cars, and other possessions. Families moved in together, saving money and creating multigenerational households. In the mid 1930s, the federal government stepped in, creating the Work Projects Administration (WPA) and the Civilian Conservation Corps (CCC) to provide jobs and the National Recovery Act, which helped workers negotiate fair wages and work hours.

National Recovery Act Quilt

Short of resources, women followed the adage "reuse, wear it out, make it do, or do without." They applied this principle to their quilting, making use of older fabrics from housedresses, older quilts, and curtains. This National Recovery Act quilt was made in 1934 by Sarah Anne Bauers. Vivian Bauers, Sarah's daughter-in-law, thinks the iron eagle symbol, which was popular in the 1930s, probably "caught her fancy." She adds that her father-in-law, a comptroller for the DM & IR Railroad in Duluth, dabbled in local politics, and that might have influenced Sarah's choice as well. Before her marriage, Sarah worked as a milliner. She was an avid gardener, expert flower arranger, and a thrifty quilter. Vivian is also thrifty, using fabric her grandmother saved to make lap robes for Lutheran World Relief.

**Original National Recovery Act Quilt | DATE: 1934
MAKER: Sarah Anne Bauers | SIZE: 67" x 83"
OWNER: Vivian Bauers**

This quilt, which commemorates the National Recovery Act (NRA), includes appliqué and embroidery.

Central Medallion Quilt with Embroidery

"Century of Progress" was the theme of the 1933 Chicago World's Fair. Sears Roebuck & Company sponsored a quilt contest with a grand prize of $1,000. The winner was selected from more than twenty-four thousand entries. Amelia Louise Stram Greinger, who was born in 1903, received a commendation for her entry commemorating inventions and accomplishments of the previous century. Materials were scarce during the Depression years but a resourceful Amelia enlisted the help of her grandfather, Grand Rapids' first tailor, who donated fabric scraps. The Greinger family had no electricity, no telephone, and no running water. Amelia sewed and embroidered the quilt by the light of a kerosene lamp. Amelia died in 1992.

World War II

The Depression began to ease after 1935, primarily due to government support, but it was not until the advent of World War II that economic times improved. After the Japanese bombed Pearl Harbor on December 7, 1941, the United States entered a war with fronts in both Europe and the Pacific. The United States had to ramp up production of steel, engines, ammunitions, nylon, cotton, and many other products necessary for large military forces overseas. This increased production created much-needed jobs, providing people with more money, but, due to wartime rationing, fewer products on which to spend it.

As in previous wars, Minnesotans went to the aid of the country, sending women and men to all branches of the service. Those on the home front did their part, too, using ration coupons; saving string and aluminum foil; working for companies such as Minnesota Mining and Manufacturing and Honeywell in war-related industries; and providing support for their loved ones overseas. "V for Victory" became the nation's slogan.

RIGHT: **Central medallion with embroidery**
DATE: **1933** | MAKER: **Amelia Louise Stram Greinger**
SIZE: **71" x 81"** | OWNER: **Louise Lee**

Amelia was commended for her entry to the 1933 Chicago World's Fair "A Century of Progress" quilt contest.

Below: Patterns from "A Century of Progress" quilt contest, sponsored by Sears Roebuck & Company.

V for Victory | DATE: **1942** | MAKER: **Alice Viola Domier Voltz** | SIZE: **80" x 89"** | OWNER: **Alice Viola Domier Voltz**

This "V for Victory" quilt no doubt was made in anticipation of the end of World War II. Alice began quilting at age fifteen and has made more than sixty quilts.

The Post-War Boom

After World War II, Minnesota was economically healthy. Cities continued to grow, and the influx of refugees from Europe, Southeast Asia, and eventually Mexico and Africa added to the culture. Minnesotans Hubert H. Humphrey and Walter Mondale left their home state to serve as vice presidents under southerners Lyndon Johnson and Jimmy Carter. Social movements such as the Civil Rights Movement and the Minnesota-based American Indian Movement brought a new sense of political activism to the state, changing its cultural atmosphere. The post-war Baby Boom increased the state's population.

In the 1950s and 1960s, women were often expected by men and the media to be housewives, whose primary job was to care for home and family. By the 1970s, the women's liberation movement gained strength, and many housewives began to work two jobs, one for an employer and one at home. Increased income and less spare time meant women sewed less, creating a lull in quilting. More families chose store-bought bedding sets than ever before. Some women, however, never stopped quilting, and their quilts, made for special family members or to commemorate events, are cherished today by their children and grandchildren.

America's quilting renaissance began in the 1960s. A post–World War II generation was coming of age. Interested in ecological movements and recycling, this generation revived long-forgotten traditional arts and modernized them, making quilting "hip" again.

SIX-POINTED STAR QUILT

Pauline Hines Peagler, known by her quilting friends as "Miss Pauline," learned to quilt in 1937 at age seven. Her mother, Mary Willie Johnson, made all of the family's clothes and made quilts with the scraps. A thrifty quilter, Mary often used old, worn quilts as batting in new quilts. Miss Pauline, two of her sisters, and family

Above: Pauline Peagler, circa 1970, in St. Paul

friends helped her mother quilt on a frame that hung from the ceiling of their Alabama farmhouse. At night they would roll the frame up to the ceiling because as Miss Pauline explained, "We had to sleep in that room!"

Miss Pauline made this Six-Pointed Star or String Star in 1960, shortly after moving to St. Paul. Though she held down two jobs, she still found time to quilt for her enjoyment. Today Miss Pauline quilts with a group of quilters from St. Paul who call themselves the Golden Thyme Golden Girls. She is still completing the quilts her mother started decades earlier.

Six-Pointed Star or String Star | DATE: 1960 | MAKER: Pauline Hines Peagler | SIZE: 86" x 94" | OWNER: Pauline Hines Peagler

Right: Miss Pauline made this Star quilt with fabric scraps left over from clothes she had sewn.

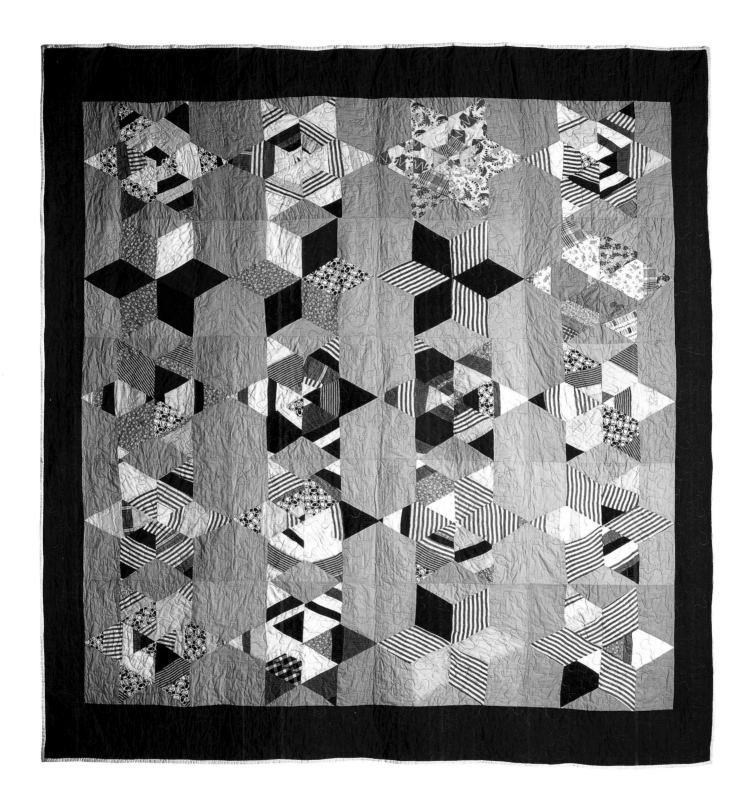

Tree Medallion | DATE: **1961** | MAKER: **Marie Pedelty** | SIZE: **97" x 105"**
OWNER: **Collection of the Minnesota Historical Society**

Marie's quilt hung in Vice President Walter Mondale's office. (Photo courtesy of Minnesota Historical Society)

Original Eagles and Shields | DATE: 1975 | MAKER: **Helen Beck Gray** | SIZE: 73" x 88" | OWNER: **Julie Kleven**

Helen designed this quilt to celebrate the country's bicentennial.

TREE MEDALLION QUILT

This Tree Medallion quilt, made in 1961 by Marie Pedelty, was exhibited in Vice President Walter Mondale's office from 1977 to 1980. His wife, Joan Mondale, chose this quilt for display as part of her campaign to elevate the status of American artists.

Marie, born in 1898, made this quilt, her first, when she was sixty-three. She simply drew the design on the muslin and covered the sketch with fabric and yarn, appliqué, and embroidery. The center depicts the oldest tree in her hometown of Madelia, Minnesota. When asked the name of the quilt she said, "The tree in Riley Smith's backyard." When she finished it, Marie presented it to her granddaughter as a gift; however, her teenage granddaughter wasn't interested in quilts and left it with Marie. When Joyce Aufderheide of New Ulm was attracted to the quilt and offered to buy it, Marie was happy to see it go to someone who

loved quilts. She said her pleasure was in the therapy of making it, not in having it. Marie died in 1986.

America's Bicentennial

Celebration of the United States' bicentennial in 1976 inspired quilters to take on patriotic projects. At that time many women and men seeking a creative outlet rediscovered the art and pleasure of quilting. Towns and organizations created bicentennial quilts, either in red, white, and blue or featuring scenes from their communities.

The bicentennial also gave Americans the opportunity to rediscover their own community and family history. Communities organized festivals, fairs, and parades to celebrate the event. "Bicentennial Minutes," which featured Revolutionary War history, aired on national television. Teachers and students delved into books and pamphlets published by local historical societies.

ORIGINAL EAGLES AND SHIELDS QUILT

Helen Beck Gray made this bicentennial quilt in 1975, creating the pieced eagles and shields and appliquéd star design herself. Helen, who was born in 1909, was once the auditor of Sherburne County and traveled extensively. Described as strong and independent by her granddaughter, she had immense pride for her country, and this pride is evident in her bold design and bright colors. Helen died in 1993.

SPACE QUILT

Some patriotic quilts celebrated pride in discoveries beyond the boundaries of our earth. Cecile Louise Du-Frene Cowdery, born in 1909, made this space exploration quilt in 1975 for her grandson. The quilt has the official emblems of the nine Apollo space missions, a Russian patch, and the family crest. Cecile, who began quilting when she was nine years old and has made two hundred quilts, painted the emblems and pieced and tied the quilt.

Quilts in the Twenty-First Century

Today the interest in quilting has never been higher. According to the 2003 National Quilting Survey, one in seven households nationwide has a quilter. Quilting has become an economically viable industry, with the average quilter spending almost $2,000 per year on quilt-related purchases. Improvement and improvisation in quilting will continue in the twenty-first century, as more people seek to be connected through quilts. Quilters will continue to find each other through quilt guilds and professional organizations. More women and men will discover their family roots through the making of memory and photo quilts. The quilt creates a tangible connection to family, community, and self in a world increasingly characterized by the intangibility of cyberspace. Create your own connections—make a quilt.

Space symbols and family crest | DATE: 1975 | MAKER: Cecile Louise DuFrene Cowdery | SIZE: 64" x 89" | OWNER: Tim Cowdery

This is one of the approximately two hundred quilts Cecile made.

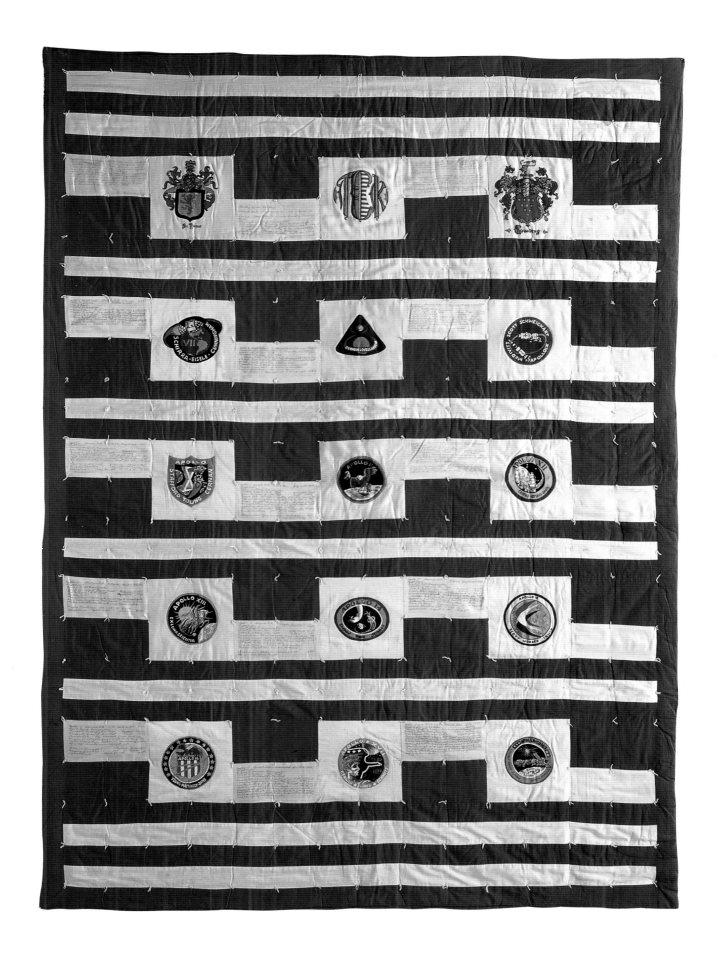

Chapter Two

Connections to Families and Friends

BY GAIL BAKKOM

The many quilts that have been documented in Minnesota and throughout the United States emphasize the importance of quilts in creating connections within families and among friends. The acknowledgment of the physical effort and emotional commitment that quiltmaking involves is manifested in the preservation of these quilts. The present owners were eager to express their emotional ties to the originators of the quilts even when they were not sure of exact histories. Their quilts have become a fabric link to their ancestors, imbued with the mysteries of the past and creating connections not only to their own family but also to history itself.

Owners expressed their astonishment at the artistic abilities and needlework skills of the quiltmakers. The delicate appliqués, combination of fabrics and colors, careful piecing of patterns, and the quilting stitches inspire them to treasure and care for these gifts. In caring for the quilt, the owner participates in the spirit of the original activity and adds another generation of memories and emotions to it. As the history of the quilts were recorded during Quilt Discovery Days, the pride in, pleasure of, and emotional attachment to these quilts was obvious.

Many of these quilts were given as gifts for special occasions, the timeless events that link families together: births, weddings, even deaths. In honoring these major events, families form bonds that meld them into a cohesive unit that supports and sustains its members. The intimate connections created by the gift quilt on these occasions make the quilt more than a mere material possession by giving it symbolic dimension, reflecting the event as well as the fam-

ily spirit. The decisions of fabric and design combine with the craftsmanship and generosity of the quilter to create an emotional response that connects the quilt, the giver, the recipient, and even future generations. Much as a stone dropped in water creates an expanding circle of ripples, so quilts produce an effect that flows from the creator to affect individuals, families, and communities.

The Crib Quilt

The crib quilt, unique because of its small size or its design inspiration, celebrates an addition to the family. Made by mothers, grandmothers, aunts, and special friends with love for a new arrival, these quilts surround the child with the quilter's warmth and generosity. Some crib quilts are reduced versions of large quilts. Others have been designed especially to entertain or enlighten. Crib quilts have frequently been "loved" to death, but some are family heirlooms that have been preserved as symbols of the quilter's importance. The Minnesota Quilt Project discovered fifty-four crib quilts, approximately one for every eighty regular-sized quilts. The disproportionate numbers may indicate that many of these gifts have disappeared.

TRIPLE IRISH CHAIN QUILT

One of the oldest crib quilts documented in Minnesota is a Triple Irish Chain, a traditional pattern that was popular throughout the nineteenth and twentieth centuries. Handpieced and handquilted, the quilt was created by a two-block repeated pattern in which three color chains intersect each other on a diagonal with

Triple Irish Chain | Date: mid nineteenth century | Maker: Unknown
Size: 38" x 38" | Owner: Hazel Lutz

A small-scale Irish Chain is executed in typical mid–nineteenth century colors.

a blank space between. It reflects the most popular color scheme of the mid nineteenth century—red and green—with an additional splash of yellow. The maker used solid color cotton and prints featuring floral and dot patterns. Quilted wreaths fill the plain blocks.

Hazel Lutz, current owner of the quilt, indicates that it was made by a paternal ancestor in Luzerne County, Pennsylvania, in the mid nineteenth century. Family history suggests that a baby was wrapped in this quilt during the battle of Gettysburg, creating a connection to an important historical event in United States history. This quilt has obviously been used, but even as the fabric disintegrates, it continues to connect Hazel to her family's history.

Made for —
Alice Arlene Kinney
By her Great Aunt —
Alice Maud Covell
In 1915.

Sunbonnet Sue Medallion Quilt

Alice Covell created this charming quilt in 1915 by for the birth of her grandniece and namesake, Alice Arlene Kinney. Alice created a center medallion quilt using figures first created in 1900 by Bertha Corbett in her self published book and made popular by the 1902 school textbook *Sunbonnet Babies Primer.* Sunbonnet Sues cavort in a circular garden of leaves and flowers, smelling and tending to the plants. Alice surrounded the garden with embroidered satin-stitched verses. Bonneted babies carry candles in the corners.

Alice Covell's parents, Frederic Brown and Maria Jerusha Andrews Brown, immigrated to Fillmore County in 1856 and then moved to Blue Earth County. Alice attended art school in Minneapolis, married Fred Covell, and settled in the Twin Cities. She painted china, watercolor landscapes, and fabric pictures. The Covells had no children, and Alice used her artistic skills to create presents for her sisters and their children. Jenelle Cunning, daughter of the child for whom this quilt was created, satin pictures and china pieces that Alice made. She also has two rag dolls embellished with embroidery that Alice made particularly for her.

Alice embroidered the following poem around the garden of Sunbonnet Sues.

These little children are happy dears
They play and pick flowers and shed no tears
So while you are sleeping so warm and light
They'll a comfort be to you, All through the night.

May your sleep be restful—my darling,
As the dark wins over the light
With the comfort children above you,
To warm you—All through the night.

And when you awake in the morning,
When the light has brought back things to sight,
May you be to your mother a comfort
As these children—to you are—At night.

Made for Alice Arlene Kinney
By her great aunt Alice Maud Covell
In 1915

Left: Quiltmaker Alice Covell

Sunbonnet Sue medallion | Dᴀᴛᴇ: **1915** | Mᴀᴋᴇʀ: **Alice Maud Brown Covell** | Sɪᴢᴇ: **51" x 53"** | Oᴡɴᴇʀ: **Jenelle Cunning, daughter of Alice Kinney**

Alice created a garden of Sunbonnet Sues for her grandniece and namesake, Alice Kinney.

Brick Wall with book pages | DATE: **1919** | MAKER:
Mary Duncan Pattison | SIZE: **45" x 47"** | OWNER:
Stearns County Historical Society

*Using a printed linen book, Mary Pattison created a quilt to
teach her grandchildren to read.*

Brick Wall with Book Pages

This Brick quilt was created by alternating red fabric and the linen pages from a story book (or two to obtain a complete alphabet) in a checkerboard pattern. The alphabet is featured through illustrations and stories. The copyright of the book is 1910. The quilt is machine pieced and machine quilted to create a strong textile meant to be used and handled by children.

Mary Duncan, born in 1840 in Perth, Scotland, emigrated to LeRoy, New York, before moving to Minnesota with her husband, William Pattison. They farmed in what is now Westwood Park. Her granddaughter, Patricia Morreim, believes that Mary was the first white woman west of the Sauk River. She was a teacher before her marriage, and her decision to remove the pages from a linen book and create an alpha-bet quilt reflects her interest in education; she wanted her grandchildren to know the alphabet before they began school. Patricia remembers her father sitting on the floor and reading the quilt to her and her siblings.

Hexagon Baskets Quilt

Hexagon quilts were particularly popular during the 1920s and 1930s, although they have been made from the earliest years of quiltmaking in this country, following a tradition of English paper piecing. While many are arranged in what has come to be known as the Grandmother's Flower Garden, other arrangements, including Hexagon Baskets, have been popular at particular times. It is unusual, however, as a pattern for a crib quilt. The fabrics in this quilt are samples from Sears Roebuck.

Although many crib quilts were created by family members, sometimes a neighbor would create a quilt for a child. Rosella Nordmeier Nusbaum was a home-maker who loved sewing and made many quilts. When her neighbor's child, Susan Cervenka, was permanent-ly disabled from bacterial meningitis in 1936, Rosella made this quilt for her. Rosella's mother helped her to quilt it. Careful workmanship, a pleasing color combination, and excellent quilting expressed Rosella's affection for the child. Susan never walked or talked, but she had a lovely smile. She used the quilt until she died at the age of eight. Mary Ruth Zweber, Susan's sister, owns the quilt and cherishes it as a reminder of Susan.

Hexagon Baskets | Date: 1936 | Maker: Rosella Nordmeier Nusbaum, quilted by Katherine Nordmeier and Rosella | Size: 42" x 50" | Owner: Mary Ruth Cervenka Zweber

Rosella Nusbaum made Hexagon Baskets for her neighbor's child.

Gay Nineties appliqué crib kit | **DATE: 1930s** | **MAKER: Ardell Brosia Kidder Findley** | **SIZE: 41" x 66"** | **OWNER: Eleanor Amidon**

Ardell's fine workmanship enhances her charming transportation-themed quilt.

GAY NINETIES KIT QUILT

Appliqué kit quilts became popular in the second quarter of the twentieth century, when many different styles were produced and sold. Charming theme-based crib quilts, such as this Gay Nineties quilt, emphasized children's story book characters, poems, or old times. This trend differed from the nineteenth century crib quilts, which were smaller versions of traditional patterns or original designs.

Ardell Findley used kits to create crib quilts for several of her children. The owner of this quilt is not sure which quilt was made for which child, but she received two crib quilts from her mother, Elsabeth Amidon, who was Ardell's daughter. Each quilt was

created in a similar style but with different subjects. This charming and well-designed kit, beautifully executed by Ardell, presents a nostalgic look at 1890s transportation methods, including boat, train, balloon, bicycle, and horse-drawn cart. Children and a church complete the scene. With its cheerful faces and bright colors, the quilt brings a happy atmosphere to a child's bedroom. Eleanor preserves these quilts as a link to her mother and grandmother.

CRAZY QUILT

Our documentation records indicate that Crazy quilts were the most popular style of the late nineteenth and early twentieth centuries in Minnesota. It is possible, however, that these quilts tended to last longer than others as they were not used as extensively or because their fabrics, which tended to be silks, satins, velvets, and wool, were not laundered as frequently. A Crazy style quilt is an unusual choice of pattern for a crib quilt in any time period, but the decline of the popularity of Crazy quilts by 1945 makes this quilt rare.

Carrie Rosaasen chose this pattern for her great-grandson, Glen Mindel. The quilt, made of pastel acetate satin, is a lovely arrangement of colors accented by embroidery. It pays homage to the earlier Crazy quilt style, but Carrie imbued it with a mid-twentieth-century feeling by her selection of fabric and color. A notation in Glen's baby book says that he received it in 1945. Glen remembers that he was not allowed to play with his quilt—although he was tempted. He, like most children, loved the feeling of the smooth, silky fabrics. Certainly his mother's cautious handling of the quilt has contributed to its excellent condition. The quilt is especially treasured by Glen and his wife, Dianne, because they share common ancestors.

Carrie, born in Norway in 1869, emigrated to the United States and married Lars Rosaasen. They farmed near Sacred Heart, Minnesota, while raising ten children. She made many quilts, and two of her daughters also became quilters.

Crazy crib | DATE: **1945** | MAKER: **Carrie E. Fagerlie Rosaasen** | SIZE: **50" x 50"** | OWNER: **Glen R. Mindel**

Carrie Rosaasen created an unusual Crazy quilt for her great-grandson.

Hattie Sidle and Edwin Roswell Barber received this quilt for their marriage in 1872.

The Wedding Quilt

Marriage is a ritual of family life. It provides for the expansion and continuity of the family and has been a joyous occasion celebrated throughout civilization. Wedding quilts express affection for and acceptance of the couple and impart an implicit blessing on the union. As the young couple begins their new life, the quilt is part of their most intimate time together, and is a reminder of their commitment to each other and to their community. These quilts are often treasured, used sparingly, and passed to the next generation of the family, creating a fabric link infused with history and affection.

Broderie Perse Quilt

The oldest wedding quilt documented in Minnesota was not created here. It is a Broderie Perse quilt, most commonly made in the eastern United States. To create Broderie Perse, quilters cut out individual pieces of a patterned fabric, rearranged them into a new pattern, and appliquéd them to a simple background cloth. A fabric called chintz was frequently used for this appliqué. "Chintz referred to a glazed cotton cloth typically printed with large-figured, polychrome designs of flowers and blossoming branches."[1] During the sec-

ond quarter of the nineteenth century it was the most expensive cotton fabric on the market and was at its peak of popularity. By cutting, and therefore extending, the expensive chintz, a small piece could create a much larger quilt. In this example, the creator used approximately five different chintzes to create a very complex medallion-style quilt. No two elements are exactly alike; detailed study shows that the same pieces were recombined in a number of different ways.

A clue to the quilt's origin is its large size, a characteristic of quilts from the East in the first half of the nineteenth century. Walter Sidle gave this quilt to his niece, Hattie Sidle, and her husband, Edwin Roswell Barber, for their marriage in 1872. Hattie was the daughter of Henry Godfrey Sidle, the founder of the First National Bank of Minneapolis. Edwin Barber was the son of Daniel Barber, president of the Barber Milling Company and owner of the Cataract Mill (the first mill on the west side of the Mississippi River in Minneapolis). It is not known if Walter actually lived in Minneapolis or if he sent the quilt from the Philadelphia area where the Sidles originated. Katherine Barber Boxnton, daughter of the bride and groom, gave this quilt to the Hennepin History Museum in 1958.

Broderie Perse | Date: c. 1840 Maker: Unknown | Size: 108" x 108" | Owner: Hennepin History Museum

A beautiful East Coast quilt was given as a wedding gift in Minnesota.

Tulip, flower, and heart appliqué | DATE: 1891 MAKER: Unknown | SIZE: 62" x 78" | OWNER: Kandiyohi History Museum

Appliquéd tulips celebrate the wedding of Andrew Anderson and Sarah Wokken.

TULIP, FLOWER, AND HEART APPLIQUÉ

Typical of many appliqué quilts from the late nineteenth century, the fifteen-inch quilt blocks of this quilt are handappliquéd but machine joined to create the top. Additional appliquéd daisies are centered over the joins of the block seams, and the picket fence border is machine pieced. The dye change in the green of the quilt, caused by fugitive synthetic green dyes, which first appeared in the 1870s, was common to fabric during the last quarter of the nineteenth century and appears frequently in quilts from this period

Although the creator of this wedding quilt, preserved at the Kandiyohi History Museum in Willmar, is unknown, the happy recipients were Andrew M. Anderson and Sarah Wokken. The folk quality and color of this charming piece indicate a Germanic influence, and the bride's name reinforces that assumption.

CORAL BELLS APPLIQUÉ QUILT

There are times when the best laid plans simply don't work out. Della Biiser Atz chose a charming tulip pattern from a farm magazine to make an appliqué quilt for her only son, Howard, in the hope that he would find a wife. She worked hard on the farm and quiltmaking was more of a necessity than a hobby, but in Howard's quilt she showed a whimsical side. Lines of alternating coral bells play diagonally across the quilt. The hardship of the 1930s meant that Della was unable to buy all the fabric for the quilt at one time, and she was unable to match green fabrics exactly; the resulting interplay of greens creates visual energy. Della's plan did not succeed. Howard never married and the quilt has not been used.

Della's parents were early settlers in Minnesota. Her father, George Biisser, was born in Watonwan County in 1859. His father, William, emigrated from

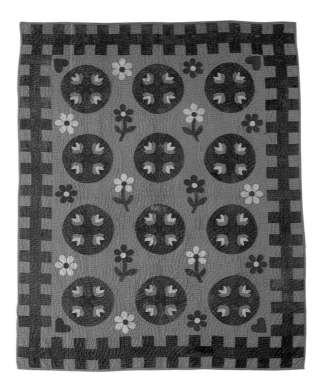

Alsace, a border province that has belonged to both France and Germany, in the early 1830s; he died while serving with the Eleventh Infantry Regiment of Minnesota in the Civil War.[2] Della's mother, Frances Mosser, was born in Madelia in 1862. Frances and George were married in February 1887, and Della was born in December of that year. Della graduated from high school and taught in rural schools until she married Henry Atz in 1914.

This appliqué quilt has become a prized possession of Ruth Stephens, reminding her of her grandmother, Della, and her uncle, Howard. She says "Howard was our favorite bachelor farmer uncle. He had a great sense of humor, but being from stoic German stock, he hid it well."[3]

Coral Bells appliqué | DATE: 1934 | MAKER: Della Biisser Atz | SIZE: 58" x 80" | OWNER: Ruth Stephens, granddaughter

Della made this delightful coral bells appliqué quilt for her son's wedding.

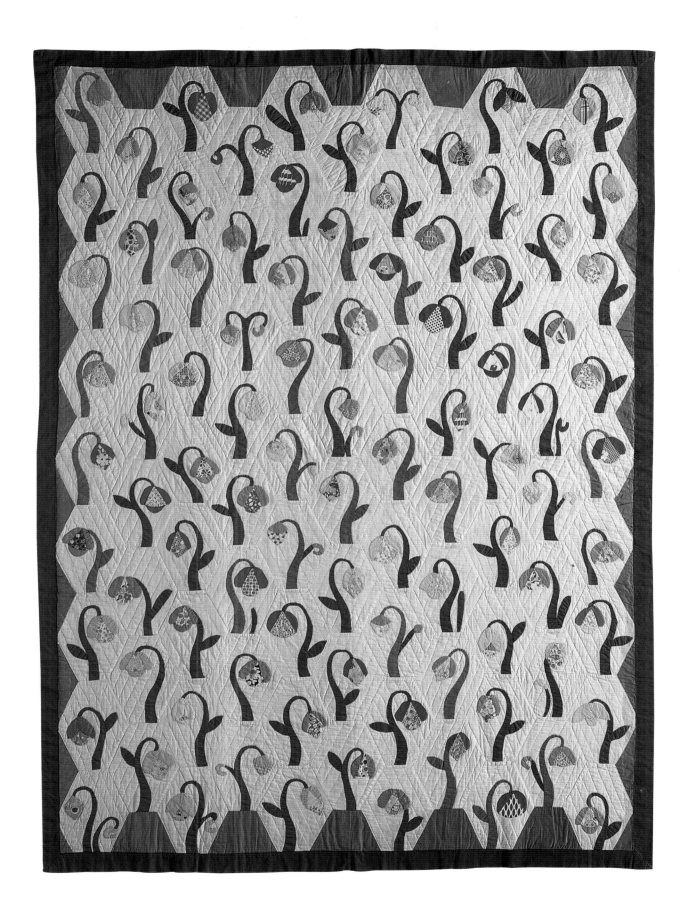

Weddings Through the Ages appliqué | Date: Begun 1949 | Block maker: Lois Jean Ward Stadler; assembled and quilted by Phyllis Thieman, sister, and Rita Grierson, niece | Size: 61" x 100" | Owner: Lois Stadler

The appliquéd design, called "Weddings Through the Ages," was designed by Marion Cheever Whiteside.

Bridal Quilt

This bridal quilt was a pattern that Lois Stadler purchased after seeing an article in the February 1949 issue of *Ladies Home Journal*. The blocks, designed by Marion Cheever Whiteside, depict marriage in different cultures and times.[4] Romanticized Egyptian, Greek, Roman, Gothic, Elizabethan, and Jewish weddings are depicted in the main part of Lois's quilt, as well as in the detail picture. A small verse accompanies each picture. An additional five "weddings" were included in the pattern but not in the finished quilt. The appliqué is quite detailed.

Lois intended to make the quilt as a gift for one of her two younger sisters, whomever married first. "But it was difficult to do despite what the article said (only a few hours per square) and this was her first attempt at making a quilt."[5] She set it aside, and her sister, Phyllis Thieman, offered to finish it for her. Phyllis, however, became busy with six young children

and didn't find the time to do it. Eventually she and her daughter put it together, deciding to set just the already finished blocks instead of including all thirteen blocks in the pattern. Small wonder that a beginning quilter was discouraged by this task, but it is easy to see why she was charmed by the article. The detail photo is described in that article as follows:

The famous Seventh regiment formed the sworded aisle For brides in fairest white—an eighteen-hundred style.[6]

Pot of Tulips Quilt

Tulips have been a popular appliqué motif in the twentieth century, and quiltmakers have added many variations to the repertoire from earlier times. In *Encyclopedia of Appliqué*, Barbara Brackman includes 106 different patterns with either tulip in the name or a tulip visual representation. Emma Anderson's Pot of Tulips contrasts the strength of the checked baskets with the soft pastels of the tulips,

Emma's parents immigrated to Martin County in 1885, and she was born in 1887. She married a farmer, Hjalmer Anderson, in 1907. She was always busy, sewing all the clothes for her family. "She loved to have visitors and I went to her house often," says her granddaughter, Marlene Mielke in a letter to the Minnesota Quilt Project. "I remember lots of fabric pieces, pins, needles, and the sound of her sewing machine going full speed. . . . She kept a lot of her quilts and the rugs she made upstairs in one of the spare bedrooms. When company came, she would spread out all her quilts on the bed for them to admire. Of course each quilt had a note pinned to it of who was going to be the recipient of it—usually one of her 21 grandchildren."[7]

Emma Anderson made two quilts for each of her six children and one for each of her twenty-one grandchildren. This Pot of Tulips was made as a wedding gift in the 1950s for granddaughter, Marlene Mielke, daughter of Gladys Anderson Swanson. Marlene treasures her quilt as she treasures the memories of her grandmother.

Pot of Tulips
Date: **c. 1955**
Maker:
Emma Mathilda Forstrom Anderson
Size: 70" x 84" | Owner:
Marlene Swanson Mielke

Emma used checkered baskets for her pastel tulips.

Tulips | DATE: **1960** | MAKER: **Mary Wagner Ludwig** | SIZE: **66" x 82"** OWNER: **Rosanne Flick**

Mary chose an unusual color scheme for an unusual Tulips pattern.

TULIPS

The Minnesota Quilt Project found approximately 1,100 appliquéd or pieced and appliquéd quilts among the 4,000 quilts recorded. Tulip patterns account for forty-four of these. This unusual pattern is not found in *Encyclopedia of Appliqué*, but it does reflect the design sensibility of the mid twentieth century.

Even nonquilters have wished to establish the bonds that a gift of a quilt can generate. Dorothy Flick, mother of Paul Flick, had this quilt made for her son and prospective daughter-in-law, Rosanne, as an engagement gift. She purchased the quilt from Mary Ludwig, a neighbor known for her quilting. When Dorothy was living with Rosanne and Paul in her later life, she loved to have this quilt on her bed at Christmas time.

Mary Ludwig was born in 1894 at New Market and lived most of her life on a farm near Fairbault. It was her practice to do chores in the morning and then spend her time quilting. She made and sold many quilts, continuing work into her nineties. Her choice of a red and green color scheme, traditional in the nineteenth century, is an unusual one for a tulip quilt in 1960.

EMBROIDERED FRIENDSHIP QUILT

Each one of the red and white chained blocks is inscribed with names or symbols that had specific meaning to the bride and groom. The reversal of the normal red on white color scheme to white on red adds visual strength to this quilt. It also "updates" the use of embroidery, which is more typical of early-twentieth-century quilts.

Kathryn Niemann and Donald Sitter asked friends and family to contribute blocks for a quilt to celebrate their marriage. Family friend Helen Kelley assembled the top, and after the wedding friends held quilting bees to complete the quilt. Kathryn explained, "We had experts and novices working on the hand stitching, which provided the charm, love, and memories stitched into the final product."[8] Helen's settings draw attention to each block while creating a pleasing overall pattern. As they preserve this quilt, Kathryn and Donald maintain a tangible reminder of their connection to their friends and family, who wished the couple a life of happiness through their stitching.

The Memorial Quilt

Memorial quilts have been made to mourn the death of relatives and friends, particularly in the second half of the nineteenth century. While they have never achieved the popularity of friendship quilts, we have seen a surge in memorial quilts in recent years, including AIDS quilts, 9/11 quilts, and Columbine quilts. The making of memorial quilts has become a way for the quilting community to reach beyond its immediate family and connect to the larger world.

Historical memorial quilts usually commemorated a familial relationship between the quiltmaker and the deceased. One Minnesota memorial quilt was the result of a doctor telling a young mother who had lost two children within a week to get a project to keep her occupied. Another was made by two sisters, who worked together to create a remembrance of their mother after her death. Stitching love and loss into a physical object allows quiet time and space for healing while creating a physical symbol of that lasting relationship.

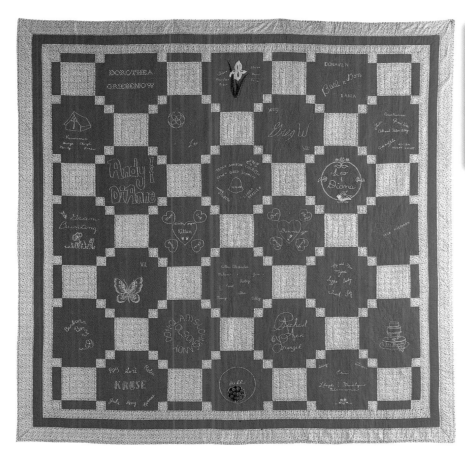

Embroidered friendship quilt | Date: 1975 | Makers: **Friends and family of Kathryn and Donald Sitter** | Setting: Helen Kelley | Quilting: 89" x 89" | Owner: **Kathryn and Donald Sitter**

Family and friends joined forces to celebrate Kathryn and Donald Sitter's wedding with a friendship quilt.

MABLE'S QUILT

There is no more wrenching event in family life than the death of a child. Rachel Swartz worked through her grief over the death of Mable, her eight-year-old daughter, by incorporating the fabric from Mable's aprons into a quilt. Mable had only two dresses; she wore aprons to help keep them clean. Rachel worked the blue and green check, plaid, and stripes of every-day aprons and red fabrics of Sunday aprons into a quilt known as "Mable's Quilt. This pattern was referred to as "Autumn Leaf" in the *Rural New Yorker* in 1931.[9] Whether the pattern name was familiar to Rachel as she made her quilt in 1895 is not known, but it certainly would be an appropriately named pattern to choose for this melancholy memorial. Mable's grave marker is still standing in Coesse, Indiana. It states:

> *Mable D., Daughter F. M. & R. A. Swartz*
> *Died Feb. 10, 1895, Aged 8 Y's 29 D's*
> *Our darling one hath gone before*
> *to greet us on the blissful shore.*[10]

Mable's quilt has been cherished by two generations. Mable's sister, Naomi Swartz Bodenhamer, received the quilt from her mother. Having been born in 1909, after Mable's death, Naomi valued the quilt for its memories of both her mother and the sister she never knew. When Naomi died in 1998, her son Fred Bodenhamer and his wife Faye, an avid quilter, inherited the quilt. They are honored to be the caretakers of this family memorial.

Recognition Quilts

Quilts are given as gifts to family members or friends to acknowledge special occasions, such as birthdays, graduations, or housewarmings. Friends or strangers may give quilts to victims of natural or manmade disasters, such as fire, flood, or (in Minnesota) tornados; the quilts offer physical warmth and comfort. Simple affection may also prompt these thoughtful presents. Whatever the reason, quilts form a link between the giver and the recipient, expressing the relevence of one to the other. In making a gift quilt, a quilter imbues it with his or her own personality, love and appreciation for the recipient. The quilt becomes a tangible symbol of their unique relationship.

SPIDER WEB QUILT

This quilt, a variation of the Spider Web pattern, is pieced with a black fabric in the center of the diamond and with multiple string piecing on both ends. It is unusual because the black fabric seems to create a setting

Above: Mable's school workbook rests on her memorial quilt.

Autumn Leaf | DATE: 1895 | MAKER: Rachel A. "Bertie" Sines Swartz | SIZE: 66" x 82"| OWNER: Fred and Faye Bodenhamer

Left: Aprons and pinafores supplied the fabric for this memorial quilt.

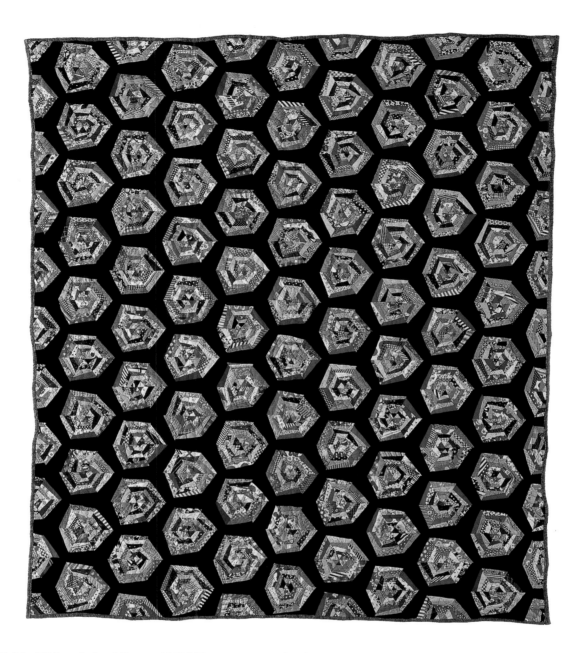

Spider Web variation | Date: 1958 | Maker: Lavina Tooker Spangenberg (1868–1961) | Size: 72" x 82" | Owner: Patricia Hobson Curran, great-granddaughter

Lavina, at age ninety, created this quilt as a birthday present for her granddaughter, Lavina Edlund Hobson. Great-granddaughter Patricia Hobson Curran now owns the quilt.

pattern but is actually the center of the block. A lively multiple-scrap quilt, it was pieced both by machine and by hand. It is handquilted in the Baptist Fan pattern.

In 1958, at the age of ninety, Lavina Spangenberg made this quilt as a birthday gift for her granddaughter, Lavina Eklund Hobson. Lavina was born in New York State, came to Minnesota in a covered wagon, and settled in the St. Cloud area. Her granddaughter and namesake, Lavina, has told Patricia, her daughter, that she remembers her grandmother making Texas Star quilts for Twin Cities clients in the 1930s. They supplied the materials and she did the sewing and quilting—earning $25 per quilt.

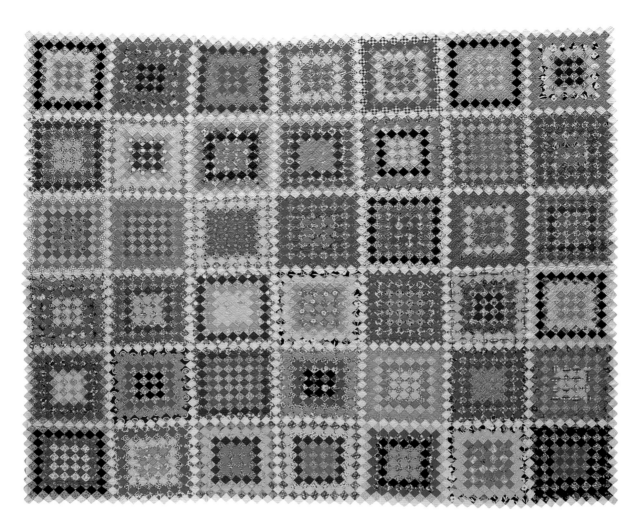

Many Trips Around the World | DATE: **1944** | MAKER: **Maud Goff Hamp (1868–1961)** | SIZE: **90" x 109"** | OWNER: **Marilyn Hanks Wells**

Maud used family clothing scraps to create a graduation quilt.

MANY TRIPS AROUND THE WORLD QUILT

During World War II, gas rationing was a fact of life. It presented difficulties for those living on farms who needed to transport their children to high schools in nearby towns. Ethel and Howard Hanks solved this problem by having their children stay with a friend, Maud Hamp, in Mapleton, Minnesota. Maud had no children and the four Hanks children became her surrogate family, staying with her during the week and returning home to spend the weekend with their parents. Marilyn, one of those children, does not think that her family paid much money for this wonderful service, but they did bring milk, eggs, meat, and baked goods from the farm each week as they returned. Maud created a quilt for each child as they graduated from high school: Fred in 1941, Bruce in 1942, Marilyn in 1944, and Lorraine in 1945. Marilyn's quilt, created from scraps of her own childhood clothing and that of other family members, is a Multiple Trip Around the World. Maud used just under five thousand one-inch-square patches to create this quilt, all handsewn. Is it any wonder that Marilyn cherishes the quilt, a symbol of the care and affection shown to her by a family friend?

Eight-Point Star Quilt

Moving into a new home is an exciting event in any woman's life. Grace Haack created this quilt as a housewarming gift for her sister, Deanne Remes. Using her skill as a quiltmaker, Grace helped her sister to celebrate her good fortune and bring the warmth of family into her new home. Grace learned to quilt at the age of ten in 4-H, and her mother encouraged and helped her. She has made many quilts in her life for family and friends and used her skill as a source of income. The Star quilt exhibits her precise machine stitching and her color coordination within a multiple-scrap framework. It is handquilted.

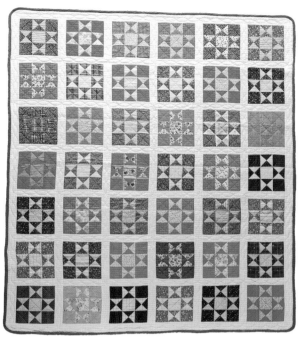

Eight-Point Star | DATE: 1968 | MAKER: Grace Ann Bohnsack Haack (1920–) | SIZE: 90" x 105" | OWNER: Richard Remes

An Eight-Point Star quilt served as a housewarming present.

Broken Dishes Quilt

Quilts have often been given as gifts during times of tragedy. Eileen Frisell's family home was destroyed by a fire in 1968. It was a subzero night near Ely, Minnesota, and the family escaped in their pajamas, losing all their possessions. In the 1940s, Eileen's grandfather, Halvar Berg, had a farm near Cyrus, Minnesota, and the wool from his sheep had been used as batting by a group of quilters in the area. One of these wool-batted quilts was donated to Eileen's family after the fire, providing not only physical warmth but also a connection to her grandfather. Annette Riley inherited the quilt from her mother. While it is plainly a utility quilt, it has style and artistic integrity. The quilt continues to remind the family of a community of quilters concerned about their welfare.

Broken Dishes variation | DATE: c. 1945 | MAKER: Mrs. Snipen and others | SIZE: 67" x 85" | OWNER: Annette Frisell Riley

Quiltmakers gave this quilt as a gift of warmth and comfort after a disastrous fire.

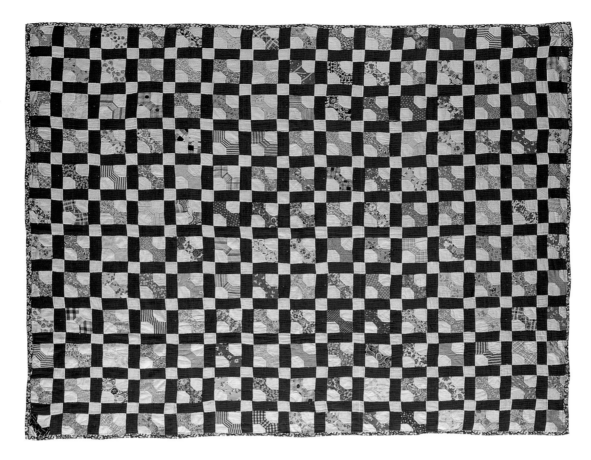

Bow Tie | **DATE: c. 1947** | **MAKER: Maria Kibbee Nichols (1860–1951)**
SIZE: 67" x 85" | **OWNER: Verly Burke Holty**

Maria made similar Bow Tie quilts for both of her great-granddaughters.

Family Quilts

Quilts are also gifted to family members as a simple demonstration of affection and the desire to create physical connections. They may be given immediately upon completion or stored to be given at some later date. Quilts are also passed to following generations by members of the family as a way to remember the quiltmaker. Whenever the gift is given, a relationship is created and sustained by the association of the quilt with its maker.

BOW TIE QUILT

Among the 1,372 quilts (plus more than one hundred baby quilts) that Maria Kibbee Nichols made was one that was a gift for her great-granddaughter, Verly Holty. Verly received her Bow Tie quilt around 1947. She has used it on her bed for many years. Her sister received a similar quilt from Maria, with green sashing instead of blue.

Maria Kibbee, daughter of Lucius Kibbee (1812–1880) and Lettie Boucher (1825–1880), was born in 1860 and came to Iowa with her husband, George, in 1879. They lived in many places during their life together, including several locations in Minnesota, Washington State, and Chicago, Illinois. When George died in 1941, Maria returned to Minnesota to live with her daughter, Gladys Gruver. Throughout her life, she made quilts and knitted mittens. "I give the quilts I make to missions, orphanages, poor people or persons burned out. Creed or color makes no difference to me. I give them to people of any church denomination and I like to help anyone who needs it," she said.[11] Several newspaper articles have been written about her generous work, and her family is justifiably proud of her good deeds.

NOSEGAY OR BRIDE'S BOUQUET QUILT

Blanche Jackery Jansen gave this quilt to Alice Hesch, her daughter, around the time of Alice's wedding in 1949. Alice didn't remember it as a wedding present; it was just a gift, although the pattern is known as "Bride's Bouquet." The use of the typical 1940s solid blue for the cones and flower centers creates a secondary pattern, adding interest to the quilt.

The early years of Blanche's life were hard. She was orphaned as a young child in Ohio when her parents died in a flood. She lived in a New York orphanage until she was put on an "orphan train," which stopped along its route to drop off children to waiting families. Blanche was adopted by a farm family in the St. Cloud area and was required to work very hard. In 1919, she married Barney Jensen and raised six children, while helping Barney with his farm. One of her pleasures in life was quilting, and Blanche gave quilts to all her children, grandchildren, and many friends. Alice's son John Hesch and his wife, Eileen, a quilter herself, treasure the quilt today as a connection to John's mother and his grandmother.

Nosegay or Bride's Bouquet | Date: c. 1949 | Maker: Blanche Jackery Jansen (? –1989) | Size: 67" x 86" | Owner: Eileen and John Hesch

Blanche made "Nosegay" for her daughter, Alice.

Quiltmaker Rosalia Backes

Contained Crazy | DATE: c. 1940 MAKER: Rosalia Maria Becker Backes (1904–2003) | SIZE: 71" x 85" | OWNER: Elaine Willenbring

Rosalia used scraps from her local milliner to create this contained variation of a Crazy quilt.

CONTAINED CRAZY QUILT

A quilt can be a long time in the making. Rosalia Backes began this quilt in the early 1930s, obtaining the materials for it from the local milliner, Mary Feldhege, who was willing to share the scraps from her cuttings. Rosalia estimates that it took her about ten years to finish this quilt, which is made of velvets and corduroy. The jewel tone plush fabrics, the bold embroidery, and the black sashing, arranged as an over and under ribbon pattern, make this a textually rich quilt. Although the family thinks of it as a Crazy quilt, it is highly organized and well planned. Only the materials and the embroidery place it in the Crazy quilt category.

Rosalia began quilting in the 1920s and has made some thirty quilts. She lived all her life in Richmond, Minnesota, as did her parents, Margareth Weber (b. 1875) and Joseph Becker (b. 1869). Rosalia's grandmother, Barbara Meyer, emigrated from Germany in 1853 at the age of thirteen, settling with her family in Iowa. When Barbara and her husband, Claudius Weber, were married, they moved to Richmond, Minnesota, where they founded the Richmond Brewery. Barbara's daughter, Margareth, was a dedicated quilter who taught Rosalia to quilt—and she taught her well. This quilt has been given to Elaine, Rosalia's daughter, who carries on the family quiltmaking tradition.

BRIDAL BOUQUET QUILT

This Bridal Bouquet quilt kit was advertised in January 1940 *Needlecraft—The Home Arts Magazine*: "Order now, Bridal Bouquet quilt $2.98. Bleached Sheeting size 81 by 100, stamped with appliqué and quilting patterns, stamped appliqué patches in pink, blue, yellow, green and lavender and pink and green bias binding for edging."[12] Ardell Findley choose to bind her quilt in the pink bias binding.

Ardell made several kit quilts, executing them with skill in both appliqué and quilting. This quilt was a gift for her daughter, Elsabeth Amidon, and was inherited by Elsabeth's daughter, Eleanor Amidon, upon her mother's death. Eleanor believes this quilt was made in the late 1930s, which suggests this pattern ran in the magazine for a period of time. It was one of the last quilts that Ardell made, and Eleanor preserves it as a link to Ardell and Elsabeth.

Bridal Bouquet | DATE: **c. 1938** | MAKER: **Ardell Brosia Kidder Findley (1882–1943)** | SIZE: **79" x 97"** | OWNER: **Eleanor Amidon**

The kit for Bridal Bouquet appeared in the January 1940 issue of Needlecraft—The Home Arts Magazine.

Since the Log Cabin pattern appeared in the mid nineteenth century, all its variations have been popular. Cora Ormseth chose this pattern for her gift to Dennis Ormseth and his wife, Turid, who reside in Minnesota. Cora learned quilting from her mother and made more than one hundred quilts. The skills Cora developed during her lifetime are evident in her Pineapple quilt. The choice of fabric pattern, color contrast, and the strategic center blocks make a very graphic quilt.

Cora was born of Norwegian parents in Pelican Rapids in 1901. She attended St. Olaf College and chose teaching as her career. Accepting a job at a one-room schoolhouse in Montana, she met and married Leonard Ormseth and settled in that state, raising three sons. She enjoyed using fabrics that had meaning and told stories, such as uniform wool from World War I or fabric from clothing worn on "special" days. She also enjoyed buying old cotton dresses at home sales, preferring the effect created by the older, slightly worn fabric. Cora used her quilts throughout her home and gave some to family members. Turid and Dennis have cherished and used this quilt.

Family Quiltmaking

Not only do quilts connect families when they are given as gifts, but they also strengthen families by

Pineapple Log Cabin | DATE: c. 1960 | MAKER: Cora Halgeson Ormseth (1901–1989) | SIZE: 85" x 99" | OWNER: Dennis and Turid Ormseth

Cora created this Pineapple Log Cabin as a gift for her son and his wife.

Above: Quiltmaker Agnes Houle Dupuis

Left: Mother and daughter created this quilt from surplus World War I window flags.

Star of Bethlehem | DATE: Begun 1932, finished 1944 | MAKERS: Agnes Houle Dupuis (1887–1994) and Martha Dupuis Benke (1918–2001), quilted by Agnes, Belle, Gertrude, Martha, and Edna Dupuis | SIZE: 79" x 79" OWNER: Donna Edwards Spychalla

uniting members in a shared activity. The camaraderie that develops as sisters quilt together or as mother, daughter, and granddaughter share a common goal creates bonds that remain long after the quilt is complete. Memories of fellowship and common purpose enhance the completed quilt's value as a useful and artistic object.

STAR OF BETHLEHEM QUILT

The Dupuis family undertook a family quilt project, using surplus goods from World War I. A neighbor near their home in Centerville, Minnesota, went to a railroad auction and purchased a large box of surplus cotton window flags used by families to indicate they had relatives in the service. Knowing that Agnes Dupuis was an avid and talented quilter and would make good use of this unusual item, he gave the box of flags to her. Agnes and her daughters ripped the flags apart, washed and ironed them, and had materi-

als for four quilts. Agnes (Belle), the oldest daughter, chose a Pineapple Log Cabin pattern; Gertrude chose a Double Irish Chain, Martha chose a patriotic Star, and Edna chose a Log Cabin. Three of these have since worn out; the fourth, Martha's, has been treasured and survives. Agnes worked on each of these quilts, helping her daughters with their creations, and each daughter helped to quilt their siblings' tops.

Agnes was of French Canadian descent and learned English after her marriage in 1913. She worked as a cook in the lumber camps, specializing in doughnuts and pies. Perhaps that was what attracted Gilbert Dupuis, who worked a logging boom in Stillwater. He was known to start each meal by asking, "What's for dessert?" Agnes lived a productive 106 years. In her later years, she proudly displayed a family tree showing her ninety-one descendants. Donna, Agnes's granddaughter, values this Star quilt for its connections to her grandmother and her aunt, Martha Dupuis Benke.

BASKETS QUILT

Hazel Roemhildt brought the Baskets quilt that her mother and her sisters made for her wedding to a Quilt Discovery Day in Waseca. Each daughter in the family received a quilt of this pattern, done in a different color: one green, one blue, and the pink one that Hazel owns. Hazel's mother, Sophia, created these delicate baskets with embroidered flowers in the log house she shared with her husband, Fred Siebert, and their ten children. With her treadle sewing machine, Sophia made quilts and all the family's clothes.

Hazel Roemhildt exhibited pride in her mother's piecing and quilting in an oral interview. Asked when she began quilting she said, "When I was a little girl there was nothing else to do. You had a radio, sure, but if you didn't have money to get the battery fixed all the time, there wasn't anything else to do but read

and see what your mother was doing. And my mother made quilts—beautiful quilts."[13] Hazel thinks that she began quilting, with help from her mother at about age eight. "Mother taught us to sew by hand first. She never trusted us on the sewing machine. One sewing machine and she took very good care of that. She said you learn to sew by hand. And we did."[14] When asked about quilting with her mother and her sisters, Hazel replied, "Yes, she made quilts for us and we helped her with everything, and when we left home she saw that we had quilts, because we had helped her for years."[15] Hazel has never used this quilt; she preserves it as a connection to her family and their work together. Hazel continues the family tradition by making quilts for her children, grandchildren, and great grandchildren.

Baskets | DATE: c. 1930 | MAKERS: Sophia Christina Herbst Siebert (1869–1948) with help from daughters Ida, Eleanore, and Hazel | SIZE: 78" x 82" | OWNER: Hazel Roemhildt

Mother and daughters created this Baskets quilt together.

Checkerboard | DATE: **1931** | MAKER: **Ida Dreier Bentz and Leona Bentz Buerkle** | SIZE: **72" x 77"** | OWNER: **Marlys Bergeman**

Mother and daughter worked together on this quilt in preparation for the daughter's wedding.

BUERKLE FAMILY QUILTS

The two quilts pictured from the Bentz Buerkle family illustrate the shared experiences and family connections that quiltmaking engenders. Ida Dreier was the daughter of Fritz Dreier, who moved to Minnesota from Illinois in 1864, and Mary Ortlepp, who emigrated from Germany with her family in 1882 when she was fifteen. Mary was a prolific quilter and taught Ida to quilt. Ida also studied sewing in Minneapolis. When Ida married Albert Bentz, they moved to a farm close to Mary and Fritz. Mother and daughter quilted together and taught Leona Bentz, Ida's daughter, to quilt. The lovely yellow and white rayon quilt was made by Ida and Leona in preparation for Leona's wedding to Adolph Buerkle in 1932. It won the Sibley County Fair blue ribbon in 1952. It has been used only for special occasions and is now owned by Marlys Bergeman, one of Leona's three daughters. The girls share the seventy-five quilts from Leona's prolific quiltmaking. "About

quilting—there's nothing to it" was Leona's comment. Excerpts from her diary read:

> *Jan. 17, 1934. Elvira and Leona Sievert were over all day and helped quilt. Evening Emma S. and Mother helped.*
>
> *Feb. 7, 1934. Elvira was over all day and started to make a Star quilt. Evening I over to Sieverts to help quilt.*
>
> *March 1, 1934. I was over at my folks and helped quilt the Star quilt."* [16]

The blue and white Drunkard's Path was made by Leona with help from Ida and friends. It was a gift for her father-in-law, Emil Buerkle, and the family gave it back to her when he died several years later. Like the Checkerboard quilt, the Drunkard's Path is in the care of Marlys Bergemen.

Drunkard's Path
DATE: 1935
MAKER: Leona Bentz Buerkle with help from Ida Bentz and friends | SIZE: 82" x 88" | OWNER: Marlys Bergemen

A daughter and her mother gathered with friends to create this quilt for the daughter's father-in-law.

Below: Four generations quilt together. Shown third from left is quiltmaker Leona Bentz Buerkle, seated next to her daughter, Lois Bode, second from left.

Quilts by Men

Women are not the only people who realize the importance of quilts. Men have also been involved in quiltmaking and have used quilts as special gifts to connect families. Although male quiltmakers were not present in large numbers in the nineteenth century, they have been documented. James Marcus de LaFayette Nunnelee, a surveyor from Tennessee, designed the rose appliqué pattern worked by his wife and three daughters.[17] Edmund Bailey from Connecticut drew the designs for a whole-cloth quilt and then helped his wife, Mary Bigelow Bailey, quilt it during their courtship in 1812–1813.[18] John Young from New York created a quilt when he was seven.[19] John Marabach of Wheeling, West Virginia, a tailor, created a classic red and green appliqué quilt sometime in the mid nineteenth century.[20] The documentation of these male quilters suggests that other men created quilts, but either the quilts have not survived or, as the quilts passed through the family, the quilters' identities were not recorded and have been lost. Male quilters have been documented in Minnesota, mostly in the twen-

tieth century. The one exception shares a connection with John Marabach; both gentlemen were tailors.

HEXAGON QUILT

The earliest male quilter documented by the Minnesota Quilt Project is James Jack. His hexagon quilt was a gift to his brother, William Leslie Jack, for William's wedding in 1876. It contains scraps of cotton, wool, linen, and velvet, all in the strong, dark colors favored at this time. It was donated to the Crow Wing County Historical Society in 1976 along with an appliqué flower sampler top also believed to have been completed by James. Initials on the sampler blocks suggest that they may be friendship blocks given to him by his admirers when he left Wisconsin.

James was a ladies tailor and dressmaker of exceptional talent; he followed in the footsteps of his grandfather, Peter Jack, a tailor in Scotland. James's father, William, who emigrated to this country alone at the age of sixteen, was a boot maker. All three generations earned their living by sewing. Jack was a favorite of the ladies of Johnstown Center, Wisconsin, where he was known to have created more than eighty wedding gowns. His obituary states that he was invited to "all the afternoon teas and quiltings."[21] When his mother became ill, he came to St. Paul to care for her. After her death, he moved to Brainard to be near his brother, William.

Hexagon | Date: 1876 | Maker: James Jack (1849–1888) | Size: 72" x 78" | Owner: Crow Wing County Historical Society

Male quilter James Jack created this quilt for his brother's wedding.

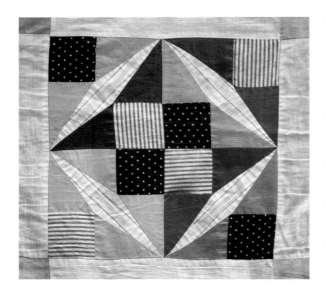

Turn of the Century | DATE: c. 1930 | MAKER:
James Gardner Bateman (1862–1953) | SIZE: 73" x 87"
OWNER: **Leona Medin**

*Skills learned as a tailor guided James Bateman's original
block creations.*

TURN OF THE CENTURY QUILT

From 1920 to 1950, some incredible male quilters received much national publicity,[22] including a chapter in Florence Petro's book, *Historic Quilts*.[23] This publicity may have suggested to other men that quiltmaking was not just a woman's prerogative. Although James Bateman created his own patterns, he must have been inspired by some contact with quilts or by a newspaper article about one of these male quilters. His daughter, Leona, remembers him sitting with a large bread board on his knee, using a ruler, square, compass, and protractor to create his unique squares. Some of these designs look like other quilt patterns, but close examination shows that his versions are more complex and reflect the work of his own geometric skills. He made three quilt tops from his wife's sewing scraps, one for his wife and one for each of his daughters, sewing the tops on a treadle machine. No two blocks in the three quilts are the same. He began his creations in the 1930s when he was in his seventies, after retiring from work in carpentry, wallpapering, and painting. His wife's quilt has been worn out, but the daughters' quilt tops remain.

Leona decided that she should do something to preserve the unique patterns her father had created and has carefully copied the sixty squares in the two tops. She has made two quilts from these patterns, one for her son and one for her niece, to continue the legacy of her father's skill. "He was a man of many talents and mostly self-taught in all areas. Patience and perfection were evident in all he did." [24] Leona speaks with pride about his skill in four-needle knitting, pie making, and bread baking. James was a lifelong resident of Michigan; his daughter brought her quilt top with her to Minnesota.

Quiltmaker James Bateman and wife Carrie

Bible history quilt | DATE: **c. 1930s**
MAKER: **Thomas and Carrie
Hovick, quilted by a friend** | SIZE:
75" x 96" | OWNER: **Alvin and
Peggy Hovick**

*Thomas Hovick embroidered this
Home Art Studio kit featuring scenes
from the Bible.*

BIBLE HISTORY QUILT

Home Art Studios published this kit in the early twentieth century. The patterns fill sixty-nine pages! Scenes from Jesus' life fill the cross; the left side of the quilt illustrates Old Testament stories, while the right side features the New Testament. Alternate blocks are quilted with crosses, and the yellow blocks are quilted with a feather design.

Thomas Hovick's quilt looks to be an exact replica of the pattern. He executed the embroidery and his wife, Helen, assembled the squares. He also embroidered two flower quilts for their daughters.

Thomas began embroidery work when he was "laid up" with a broken leg. Because it healed badly and had to be re-broken, he was unable to work for almost two years. Needing to be useful, he had Helen teach him to embroider. He gained a new skill that he would continue to use, along with his blacksmith-

ing, carpentry, wagon making, and farming. Family and newspaper accounts in Armstong, Iowa, demonstrate that he became well known for his new hobby. He created quilts, embroidered pillowcases to be sold at fundraising events, and decorated other household items. Thomas and Helen celebrated their fiftieth anniversary in 1951 with a display of their handiwork.

CARPENTER'S WHEEL QUILT

In the 1940s, Fred Check's asthma kept him indoors during the severe winter weather, and he began to help in quiltmaking for the family. This activity not only served to keep the family warm, but also united Fred and his son, Victor, in a common project. Victor had suffered severe convulsions as a child and was unable to speak. Fred and Victor quilted together until Fred's death. They made quilts for all Fred's children and grandchildren and also sold quilts to neighbors. The family estimates that they made between fifty and sixty quilts.

Fred emigrated to the United States from Skåne, Sweden, in 1910 after serving in the Swedish Merchant Marine for ten years. He had two sisters in Minnesota and came to live with them. While visiting a half sister in Walnut Grove, Fred met and married Alvida Stenberg. They remained in that area, farming and raising six children. He later entered construction and defense work before ending his career in the trucking business.

Bernice Bakker, Fred's daughter, brought her Carpenter's Wheel to Morris, Minnesota, to be documented. She is particularly attached to this quilt, which her father and brother created especially for her. She never used the quilt and has passed it on to her daughter for safekeeping.

Fred Check, front row, first from right, and Victor Check, back row, first from right, were the quilters in the family.

Carpenter's Wheel | DATE: 1958 | MAKERS: Fred (1886–1969) and Victor Check (1918–2004) | SIZE: 69" x 93" | OWNER: Rosemary Bakker

Father and son created many quilts together.

Chapter Three

Connections to Community

BY KELLY WILLIS

Throughout history quiltmakers who reside in the same area have formed groups to share their skills and talents with one another and the greater community. A quilt's connection to the community can be diverse, from the pattern idea that is shared with others, to the quilting stitches added at a quilting bee, to the sharing of the quilt with the people who enjoy seeing and owning the finished work. Though some may think of quilting as a solitary activity, quiltmakers can often relate stories about the community of people that contributed to the composition and construction of their quilt. Many owners no longer know the original reason for the specific construction or design that the maker selected, but most owners know some history related to the quilt that connects it to others. Of course there are quilts with unknown histories; however, the design, fabrics, or unique markings of the quilt itself provide a beginning of a connection to its history and to the community in which it was made. As we share the quilts documented in this book, an even greater quilting community will be tied to each quilt.

Friendship Quilts

A quilt with a close personal community connection involves family members and friends in the quilting process. Friendship quilts containing individuals' signatures, poems, quotations, or pictures were quilts with personal ties. In many cases, these quilts were gifts of friendship to someone who was moving, providing a way for quilters and friends to remain connected. The names were not the only significant part of the quilt; the quilt block may have been made of a fabric from a childhood dress, or a block design chosen to remind the recipient of the quilt of its makers. Although commonly given as a gift in parting, quilts

with names, quotes, or poems are featured in designs made for many occasions. We still see friendship quilts made today in various designs.

Before friendship quilts became popular around 1830, people kept friendship album books, blank books that friends would sign with short messages and poems. Magazines and etiquette books of the time, such as the *Godey's Lady's Book*, contained printed messages and poems that could be copied into a friend's album or onto a quilt block. Bible verses were also used in the books and on the quilts. From 1840 until 1875, friendship quilts were very popular. Popular patterns included the Chimney Sweep Block, now often called the Friendship Block. Most signed quilts contained a block design with a light-colored center fabric for the signatures; however, designs such as Nine Patch, Stars, and Baskets were also used. In general, signed quilts made before the 1830s feature embroidered or cross-stitched names.[1] In the 1840s, new inks became available that enabled quilters to write or stencil on fabrics, making a permanent inscription possible. The production of steel pen points and metal stencil name plates made writing on fabrics easier and more legible.

The period from 1840 through 1875, when friendship quilts were popular, was also the time when many families left loved ones in the East to claim land in the Midwestern states. There was rapid migration into Minnesota between 1848 and 1859. The Minnesota Census records indicated that the number of women and girls living in Minnesota increased from 2,343 in 1850 to 78,806 in 1860—a thirty-three fold increase in a single decade.[2] Since space was limited, travelers brought only the most needed items. A friendship quilt was a useful gift that could be taken on the journey to the new homestead. Many newcomers arrived with quilts that connected them to family and friends far away.

Irish Chain | **D**ATE: **1844** |
MAKER: **Margaret W. Treadwell**
SIZE: **Large quilt: 101" x 108",**
Crib quilt: 47" x 48" | **O**WNER:
Collection of Chester County
Historical Society, West Chester, PA

These 1840s crib and full-size quilts were made for a Minnesota immigrant family by a relative from Pennsylvania.

Inked inscription from one quilt block.

IRISH CHAIN QUILTS

Rachelle Ely Randall Watson, Ezekiel York Watson, M.D., and their young daughter Ellen Jane were three early immigrants, arriving in Minnesota around 1844. The Watsons were a Quaker farm family from West Chester County, Pennsylvania. Many friendship quilts originated in the West Chester County region in the mid 1840s and can be found in private collections and museums.[3] The oral family history given at the Quilt Discovery Day and dates and names in the family Bible confirm that these quilts traveled with the Watsons from Philadelphia to Minnesota. The large quilt, measuring 101 by 108 inches, is made in an Irish Chain pattern set with a double sawtooth border. The small Irish Chain quilt is 47 by 48 inches set in a grid design.

The large quilt was made for the Watsons by Ellen Jane's aunt Margaret W. Treadwell. It is an exceptional example of a friendship quilt in its pattern style and features numerous signatures and poems added primarily by relatives and family members who remained in Pennsylvania. It has inscriptions in the middle of each block written in dark ink and the date 1844 inscribed in numerous blocks.

Margaret Treadwell made the small quilt for Ellen Jane, born in 1842. The quilt features the following Bible verse:

Presented to Ellen Jane Watson
By her aunt Margaret W. Treadwell
January 1844
   "Suffer little children to come
   unto me and forbid them not for
   of such is the kingdom of heaven"
Philadelphia

Ellen Jane Watson married Luther Mendenhall in 1870. They passed down the quilts to family members, who kept them in excellent condition. Family members Betty and Maxwell Ramsland donated the quilts to the Chester County Historical Society in West Chester, Pennsylvania.

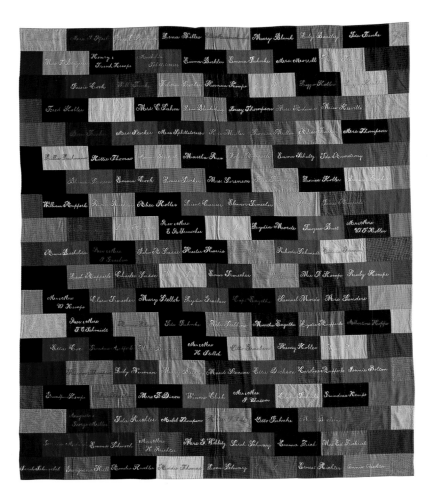

Brick | DATE: 1899 | MAKER: Unknown | SIZE: 68" x 81" OWNER: Winona County Historical Society Collection

This Brick signature quilt has 134 embroidered names.

The following poem is written in ink on the large quilt and signed by the quiltmaker:

Farewell: how that word trills the heart with emotion,
And recalls to the mind's joy are more to return,
Reviving those senses where the heart's pure devotion
Enkindled a flame that consists to ceaselessly burn.
What though it is uttered can time's separation
Efface from the memory the joys of the fast?
Lo a bliss is in prospect for whose preparation
Life's day is well spent if we reach it at last.
Philadelphia, March 27, 1844, Margaret W. Treadwell

Signature Quilts

Signature quilts were connected to the general public or a larger community, and the receiver may not have personal connection with each signer. Signature quilts were made for fundraising, for charity events, or for commemorative and presentational gifts. A presentational quilt is one presented to an individual as a thank you, farewell, or welcome gift to a prominent person of the community. In most signature gift quilts, participants shared in the signing but not always in the construction. A quiltmaker assembled the quilt blocks or top and then others signed the quilt. Sometimes the names were collected and placed on the quilt in one person's handwriting or in embroidery stitching before the quilt was assembled. The finished quilt was presented to a prominent person such as a pastor, doctor or politician, or to a social, political, or religious group. Many of these quilts have remained in good condition because family members did not use them because they knew the signatures were important. As time passed, the family members who did not feel a connection to the signers may give these quilts to county historical societies because the quilts' main connections are with the communities where they originated.

BRICK SIGNATURE QUILT

This Brick design signature block quilt is from the Winona County Historical Society collection. The 134 names are embroidered on individual blocks. Many of the names belong to families who lived in the Winona County area. The one dated block includes the name Mrs. Will J. Vetter, 1899. The quilt is made of primarily dark multicolored cotton and wool fabrics with no batting, and each block measures 4 by 8 inches. The block set in this design is a very easy set for quick construction. Unfortunately, this is an example of a quilt that has outlived its original intent and makers; one can only speculate as to who the makers were and their reason for making this Brick quilt.

OAK PARK LUTHERAN CHURCH SIGNATURE QUILT

When Ralph Lehart, the minister to Oak Park Lutheran Church in Clearwater, Minnesota, was appointed to another church, the women of the church made him this signature presentation quilt and gave it to him as a going away gift in 1921. The twenty-nine names of women from the church are embroidered and ink stamped on the quilt. The majority of the 13-by-13-inch blocks are made of dark and light fabrics cut in half-square triangles, with signatures in the light triangles and embroidered floral designs in the dark triangles. This friendship quilt is housed at the Clearwater County Historical Museum.

Signature presentational quilt | **DATE:** 1921 | **MAKER:** **Women of Oak Park Lutheran Church** | **SIZE:** 69" x 80" | **OWNER:** **Clearwater County Historical Society collection**

A signature presentational quilt from Clearwater County, Minnesota

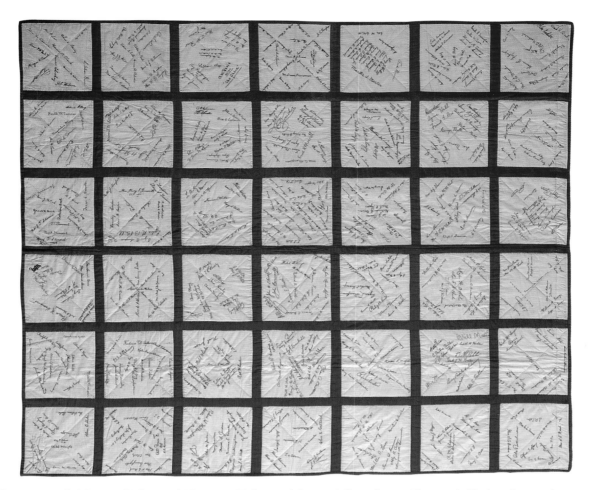

Signature quilt | DATE: Unknown | MAKER: Unknown | SIZE: 67" x 79"
OWNER: Hennepin County Historical Society collection

This simple block quilt is made exceptional with 625 embroidered names.

RED AND WHITE SIGNATURE QUILT

This signature quilt from the collection of the Hennepin County Historical Society has 625 names, embroidered in red on a white background blocks. Names are very carefully laid out and written on some blocks, and the white blocks are sashed with solid red fabric. Straight line quilting is used throughout. This is one of many beautiful quilts about which little is known. Was it made for a fundraiser, for a conference, or as a gift? Fortunately, it can be enjoyed for its visual attributes and serve as an inspiration to other quiltmakers.

These quilts were all made to remember a relationship or community connection that was important to both the makers and receivers at the time.

EMBROIDERED FLOWER PETAL SIGNATURE QUILT

This commemorative or presentational quilt, made circa 1905, was owned by Reba Post, a spiritualist minister who lived in Minnesota. The pattern used is a Sunflower variation.[4] The names of spiritual leaders are embroidered in white along the flower petals and in the sashing. Each flower center is embroidered with a name of a state or city in the United States, including Washington, D.C., Chicago, Pennsylvania, Michigan, and Iowa. Embroidered on the quilt is information about the spiritual organization. One block in the center reads "Originated 1893 Nation Spiritualists Association." On the petals, the words "1905 Officer Election" are followed by the names of the officers. This quilt is currently in the collection of the Dakota County Historical Society.

Signature quilt with Red Sunflower blocks
DATE: **c. 1905** | MAKER: **Unknown**
SIZE: **64" x 79"** | OWNER: **Dakota County Historical Society Collection**

Red Sunflower blocks provide space for numerous embroidered names on this quilt.

Quilting Groups

Quilting circles, also called quilting clubs or quilting groups, are gatherings of quilters within the local community, who meet to share their art, stories, and lives with other members. Quilting groups meet on an ongoing basis to work together on numerous quilts. Individual members may come and go throughout the life of a group, but the group will continue to meet. These groups often serve the larger community by contributing to local community charities, both monetarily and with gifts of quilts or blankets. Members also benefit from the group, as there is a fellowship that develops between quilters as they work together. Members of these groups report that they enjoy the friendship and companionship. It's not long before quilts and quilting become the background to the socializing itself. In interviews, members talked about the fellow members who have become friends, the lunches, and the parties before commenting on the hundreds of quilts the group had worked on. Minnesota quilters have been a part of these groups for many years. Boni Agee Matton ended her poem in 1989 about the Helping Hands Club (now called Helping Hands Quilters) this way:

Here we are in our sixty-fifth year
Surrounded with this love and laughter,
May it always be, as the old saying goes,
They quilted happily ever after.

As we quilt, we stitch a chain
That carries us through the laughter and pain
Of friendships lost and friendships gained.

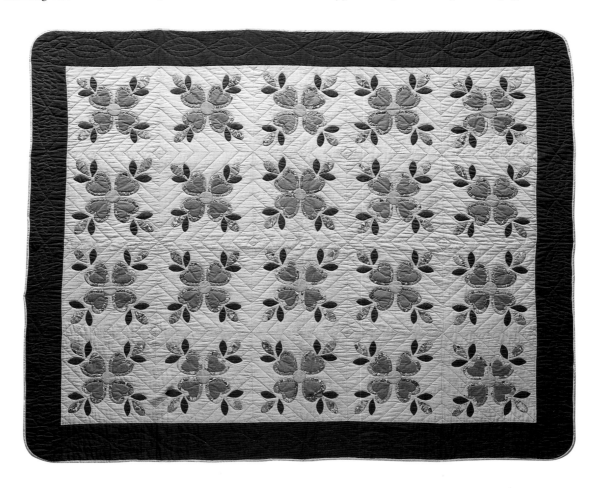

Appliqué | Date: 1967 | Makers: Helping Hands Quilters | Size: 67" x 84" | Owner: Washington County Historical Society Collection

Members of the Helping Hands Quilters made this Ohio Rose quilt.

GIVING A DEMONSTRATION ON QUILTING during the Washington Co. Historical Society tea at the museum on Saturday, June 10 are these members of the Helping Hand Quilting club. Seated: Mrs. Joseph Bruchu and Mrs. Raymond Kern. Looking on, left to right, are members: Mrs. Robert Mundt, Mrs. Fred Schlesser, Mrs. Ben Pritzel, Mrs. Roy Ogren, Mrs. Otto Wolf. The portrait on the wall is of the Reverend William Boutwell, one of the early ministers of Stillwater.

Historical Society Tea Features Quilting Bee

In spite of the inclement weather, more than sixty guests attended the Saturday afternoon Historical Society tea held at the Washington County museum on north Main street, Stillwater.

The principal feature of the occasion was a quilting exhibit and demonstration put on by the Baytown Helping Hand Quilting club which has been in active operation in the county for over 41 years. Up to the present time, the members have turned out 700 quilts, many of which have gone to needy families made destitute by fires and other disasters. At yesterday's Tea, on behalf of the club, it's president, Mrs. Ben P. Pritzel, presented to Mrs. Frank Siefert, President of the Washington County Historical Society, a beautiful Ohio Rose quilt of their own making, to be placed in the museum in recognition of the work and service of the club. Prior to the ceremony, eight members of the quilting club worked on a small quilt set up in quilting frames in the north parlor of the museum. They

ADMIRING QUILT PRESENTED TO WASHINGTON CO. HISTORICAL MUSEUM are: left to right, Mrs. Ben Pritzel of the Helping Hand Quilting club and Mrs. Otto H. Wolf, charter member. The club made the quilt, with a design called "Ohio Rose." Looking very happy to receive the quilt is Mrs. Frank Siefert, right, pres. of the Washington County Historical Society. The quilt was presented during the annual tea of the Historical Society at the Museum on Saturday afternoon, June 10.

* * * * * *

er volunteers.

Mrs. Ruth Woodworth, curator, and her associate, Mrs. Grace McAlpine, assisted by Mrs. Hattie Connors and other members of the society, acted as hostesses for the affair. A new additon to the

Connors and the whiskers a la Mrs. McAlpine. Mrs. Lurenah Stiles provided for the occasion a rare piece of actress glass containing the picture of Jenny Lind on the stem.

The museum is open for tours

Above: Members of Helping Hands Quilters, 1967

Helping Hands Quilters

One of the many Minnesota quilting groups is the Helping Hands Quilters, whose members have been meeting near Stillwater, Minnesota, since 1924. The group, originally called the Helping Hands Club, consists of nine to sixteen woman (and sometimes one man) and meets each month at a different member's house. They begin quilting early in the morning, eat lunch, and continue to quilt throughout the day. During the holidays, the group will not meet to quilt but will gather instead for a luncheon, bringing their husbands as guests. Throughout the years, they have made quilts for themselves, as gifts, and for donation to needy families. Bernadette Kauthold has been quilting with the group for twenty years and remembers, "Years ago you had to be invited into the group.

You had to know someone, a cousin or neighbor. The old timers would often watch the new quilters. No toe catchers, or people who made large stitches were asked back."[5] She estimates that the group has quilted more than eight hundred quilts.

OHIO ROSE QUILT

The women of the Helping Hands Quilters quilted this appliqué quilt in 1967. The group calls the pink and blue heart floral appliqué the "Ohio Rose Quilt," and they presented it to the Washington County Historical Society at a society tea. To make this twenty-block quilt, each club member pieced one or two blocks, and then the club gathered to do the quilting. The making of this quilt can be traced through the club's monthly meeting notes.

Jan 4, 1966: The first meeting of the new year was at Mrs. Henning's home. We spent the afternoon working on quilt blocks for a quilt. . . . [These were the Ohio Rose blocks.] We had a special meeting in Jan. to make a quilt for a family that lost their home by fire.

April 1967: The meeting of April 4, was entertained by Mrs. Madsen. We spent the day quilting. The meeting was called to order. The club will quilt a quilt for St Paul's church. We will donate our work. We are making a quilt which we will quilt at the historical society spring meeting and donate to the society to be on display. We made a quilt for a family that lost their home by fire at a special meeting at Mrs. Wolf on April 11th. . . .

May 3: The meeting for May 3rd was at Mrs. Pretzels home. We spent the day working on a quilt. [The members believe this was the Ohio Rose quilt.]

June 6: The regular June meeting on the 6th was entertained by Mrs. Pretzel. We spent the day quilting. The meeting was called to order we finished making plans to go to the historical society meeting. No other business so the meeting was closed.

July 5, 1967: The club attended the historical society tea on June 10th at which time we presented a

hand made quilt to the museum to be put on dis-
play there permanently. We also set up a small quilt
to demonstrate our method of quilting. . . . [6]

The original minutes for each quilt session are still with the club. The group said that over the years they have begun making smaller baby quilts for their grandchildren and great grandchildren. The Helping Hands Quilters celebrated their eightieth year in 2004. The following stanzas are from a poem about the quilting club by 1959 president, Arline Kern, in honor of the group's thirty-fifth anniversary party.

> *On a cold winter day in February of '24*
> *A knock was heard on Mrs. Wolf's door.*
> *'Twas Mrs. Richert who came up with a plan*
> *For neighbor women to make up this clan.*
> *Their motives were constructive as you can see*
> *For out of this gathering was born our "quilting bee."*
> *To these noble women who all said they would*
> *Each in her own gave all that she could*
> *To set a standard for this friendly club*
> *Where happy hours of sewing, chit-chat and grub*
> *Was the order of the day, but then came the time*
> *When other new members came into the line.*
> *Regardless of creed, age, status, or birth*
> *They all became members for what it was worth.*
>
> *These faithful women, we can call might fine.*
> *In this big circle we found friendship everlasting*
> *Although many of the roll have gone now into passing*
> *But their memories linger on with the work that*
> *was done*
> *To bring joy and cheer to the under-privileged one.*
> *Many quilts were made for the homeless and needy*
> *Surely provide a point—Helping Hands—was not*
> *greedy.*
> *For 35 years each month they have met*
> *To sew on a quilt—or what have you I guess.*
> *Sometimes it's been stripping feathers, hemming*
> *towels or the such,*
> *But quilting was our specialty and still is a must.*
>
> *With this reminiscing, I hope you had fun*
> *When you look back on all what was done.*
> *All wasn't gossip or this or that*

> *Once in a while our fingers worked fast*
> *To accomplish as much as it could be*
> *On a happy afternoon with this big family.*
> Arline Kern, President, February 3, 1959

Martha Circle Quilting Group

In Paynesville, Minnesota, another of the state's many groups, called the Martha Circle quilting group, meets each week as they have done for many years. No records exist from when this group originated, but the oldest record is from a list of costs for quilting in 1932. The quilters were well organized by then, making seventeen quilts that year alone. The group was originally called the "Ladies Aid," and current members believe it could have been organized when Paynesville was first incorporated in 1887. Many of the ladies learned to quilt from their mothers who were in the group. In 1969, members changed the name of the group to "Martha Circle." The group currently meets at Paynesville's Grace United Methodist Church, which added a room in the 1960s so that quilts can remain set up all the time. The quilters meet at 9 A.M. and work until 4 P.M., stopping for lunch and coffee breaks in between. In the first years, each quilter would bring a hotdish dinner to share, but as the ladies grew older they decided on sack lunches instead. Many of the older ladies can no longer quilt but still come to the meetings to talk and help with the coffee breaks. One or two quilts are usually set up at a time with eight to twelve quilters working. The group usually finishes a quilt in three to five weeks.

Members of the Martha Circle quilting group

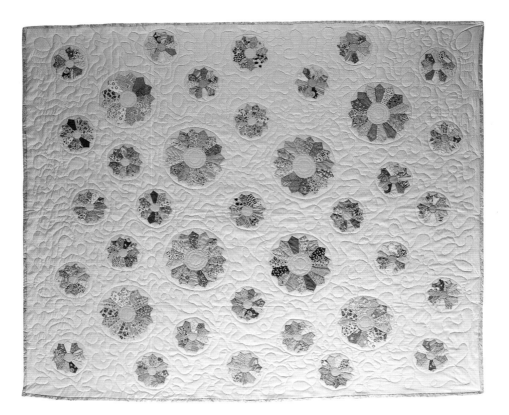

Dresden Plate | DATE: **Unknown** | MAKER: **Doris Nehring** | SIZE: **65" x 80"** | OWNER: **Private Collection**

Martha Circle members quilted this Dresden Plate quilt.

The members of Martha Circle estimate that they quilt twenty-six quilts during a year. This group receives the quilt top, back, and batting from a client and completes the quilting. They charge by the quilt size, the amount of quilting requested, and the complexity of the quilt pattern. There is always a waiting list of quilts in need of quilting. Old records from the group shows a total of fifty-eight dollars made in 1932; this would average three dollars and forty-one cents per quilt. Martha Circle also quilted for members of the group who made quilts for new babies, weddings, or special occasions. At one time they began photographing the quilts they quilted but stopped because it was too expensive to continue. Members pay monthly dues, which, along with the money made quilting, are given as donations to local charities and to the church for equipment and improvements. Some of the dues also pay for special dinners for the group. Deloris Schultz, the 2004 organizer of the group, remembers that Valentine's Day dinners of years past included herring and potatoes with a cream sauce. Deloris has seen changes in the quilts over the years she has been with the group and notes that today's quilts are much larger than they were in the past. A king- or queen-size quilt is typical now, requiring more quilting time. New polyester batting allows for less quilting, because long polyester fibers do not shift or shrink as the short fibers in old cotton batting did. Also, new technologies in cotton batting production prevent shifting, so less quilting is required on the larger quilts.

DRESDEN PLATE QUILT

Doris Nehring assembled this quilt top from Dresden Plate blocks made by her aunt, Cora Allen. The Martha Circle quilters did the quilting. Doris was a member of the Martha Circle group for many years. The multicolored fabric blocks are set with a gold centers, and the varying sizes of blocks were difficult to put together. Doris said in a local newspaper interview, "Though most of the 'original quilters' are gone, this same group has continued through the years. We seem to be a dedicated group—either that, or we are diseased with the 'quilting bug!'"[7]

Quilting Bees

Much has been written about the old time quilting bees, some of it true, some of it myth. Many quilting bees, or frolics as they are sometimes called, are described as events where women would come together to quilt during the day, and the men would join the women for a feast, lively games, and dancing far into the night.[8] A quilting bee was a very sensible and practical way to get the quilting done. A group of women together could finish an entire quilt in one day. The women who did not quilt would prepare food, and since the men and children would need to eat, it would make sense for them all to come together for a meal in the evening. Music and dancing might begin as the children played games. Merle Vollmer described her first quilting bee experiences at the Quilt Discovery Days.

Mama taught me first to quilt 'cause she belonged to a quilting party at Cordova. The ladies at the church at Cordova used to get together and quilt. Probably once a month they would go to each other's homes and quilt a quilt while they were there. And I remember having the quilting party at our house and all the ladies from this church came up in a wagon pulled with horses and then they stayed all day. My mother made dinner for them and they would quilt all forenoon and all afternoon and then go home again. They'd probably make a quilt during the day.[9]

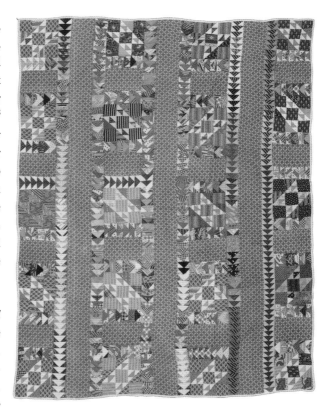

Hovering Hawks | DATE: circa 1864 | MAKER: Huldy May Horton | SIZE: 70" x 91" | OWNER: Minnesota History Center collection

Hovering Hawks Quilt was quilted at a quilting bee held in a log cabin farmhouse. (Courtesy of Minnesota Historical Society)

HOVERING HAWKS QUILT

This quilt from the Minnesota History Center Collection was made by Huldy May Horton, circa 1864. The family history accompanying the quilt stated that it was made at a quilting bee in a log cabin farmhouse located in McLeod County. The quilt is made with part of twenty blocks that are a variation of a Hovering Hawk pattern.[10] Continuing a bird theme, the quiltmaker chose a sashing design of Wild Goose Chase blocks that edge each Flying Bird block. (During the early years of settlement in Minnesota, quiltmakers would have seen many birds in and around their farms.[11]) The background strip fabric is a plaid, and the quilting follows the fabric's printed lines. Plaid fabric patterns require no quilt marking, making it easier for a group of quilters to quilt uniformly. The stitching on this quilt varies in thread color, stitch size, and stitch style. The individual blocks are a fascinating collection of fabrics, including men's shirtings in plaids and stripes, white shirting prints, and dress prints in varying shades of lavender, pink, brown, red, and orange. The quilt is in excellent condition. The colors of most of the fabrics appear new and without much fading. The quilt is entirely handpieced and handquilted.

By the late 1800s, as newcomers established and built churches in the community, the need for quilting bees decreased. Instead, women formed church quilting circles to quilt for others.[12]

PINK STAR QUILT

This quilt, which the family called the "Pink Star Quilt," is owned by Margaret Miller, who received it as a gift from her grandmother, Ethel Hicks. Ethel and her husband, Franklin Benjamin Hicks, were from the Grand Marais area, where Franklin was both the area doctor and a minister. Before living in Grand Marais, the family lived in Illinois, Iowa, and Wisconsin. Based on the owner's knowledge, the quilt was made in Grand Marais by ladies of the town and presented to the family. It has machine-pieced blocks and is handquilted. The Hunter's Star block, a combination of an eight-point star and triangle block, is nicely done in this two-color combination.[13]

Pink Star | **DATE: circa 1930s** | **MAKER: Unknown** | **SIZE: 73" x 87"**
OWNER: Private Collection

A group of ladies from Grand Marais quilted this Star quilt for the town doctor.

Minnesota State & County Fair Quilts

Minnesota fairs have long been a place where quilters can share their love of quilts with the greater regional and state community. It is at county fairs and the Minnesota State Fair that local county residents and friends gather to socialize, see exhibits, eat new foods, and, for some, have their quilts exhibited and judged. Each county in Minnesota has a county fair exhibition, and any individual can enter a quilt in a county fair. The winners from the county fair then compete at the state fair level. The quilt exhibit has been a part of the Women's Division, the category of entries made by women, since just after fairs began. Over the years the classes for exhibited quilts have had many categories, including coverlets, piecework, whole cloth, and patchwork. Classes have changed depending on the popularity of a particular quilt style. These two quilts are a small representation of the beautiful handcraftsmanship that goes into items displayed at fairs. Many

women are no doubt inspired by work they have seen at a fair.

ENDLESS CHAIN QUILT

Martha Clara Ahmann Schoenborn entered this Endless Chain pattern quilt in the Mahnomen County Fair in 1946, and it won first place. The premium for a first-place entry was four dollars. Martha pieced together this quilt in a variety of multicolored cotton fabrics from her mother's scrap bag, placing the blocks on an off-white colored background. The nine-inch-square blocks are both hand and machine pieced in a variation of the Endless Chain pattern.[14] The Endless Chain quilt is echo stitched around the chaining link piecing, with a border quilted in a fan pattern.

Martha said, "It was the first quilt that my mother, Gertrude Ahmann, taught me how to cut, assemble

Above: Quiltmaker Martha Schoenborn

Endless Chain | DATE: circa 1946 MAKER: Martha Clara Ahmann Schoenborn | SIZE: 75" x 92" | OWNER: Private Collection

This Colorful Endless Chain quilt was exhibited at the Mahnomen County Fair.

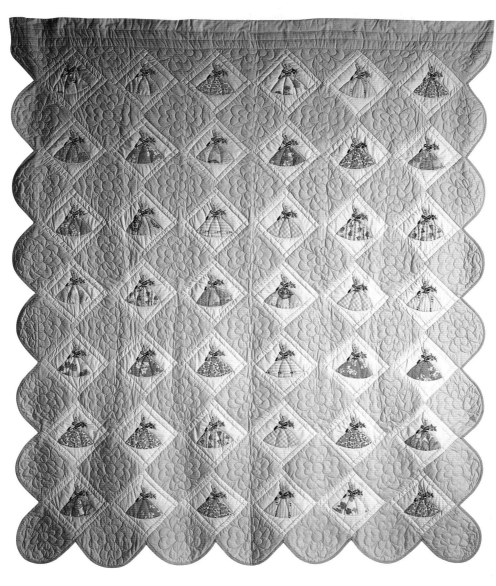

This Sunbonnet Girls quilt was exhibited at the Kandiyohi County Fair.

and sew each quilt block. She also taught me how to do handquilting by using small even stitches."[15]

Martha says she has been quilting since she was sixteen years old and has made approximately thirty quilts. She credits her mother for her teaching skills and said, "Because of my mother, I, too, enjoy the hobby of making quilts for my children and grandchildren."[16]

SUNBONNET GIRLS

Helga Maryanne Nelson Huisinga made this appliqué quilt for her granddaughter, who was getting married in 1966. In 1967, she entered it in the Kandiyohi County Fair, and it won a blue ribbon. She has entered many quilts in the local county fair during her

quilting years. Helga was born in December 1897 and lived in Minnesota her entire life. She taught school in rural Kandiyohi County for three years before she married Albert H. Huisinga. She learned quilt making from her mother. The family calls this the "Sunbonnet Girls" quilt.[17] The forty-two eight-inch-square blocks are embroidered and appliquéd with colonial ladies in dresses, mostly of printed pink fabrics. The skirts on the ladies are made with scraps left over from other items Helga had sewn. The colonial ladies blocks are set on point with an alternate solid pink fabric block and quilted in a floral design. Helga gave each of her seventeen grandchildren a quilt as a gift; she was working on the seventeenth quilt when she passed away in 1978. The family finished her last quilt.

Quiltmaker Marie Morissette at age sixteen

Nine Patch | Date: **c. 1859** | Maker: **Marie Morissette** | Size: **78" x 83"** | Owner: **Minnesota History Center collection**

In 1857, this Nine Patch won best patchwork quilt at the Forth Union Fair. (Courtesy of the Minnesota Historical Society)

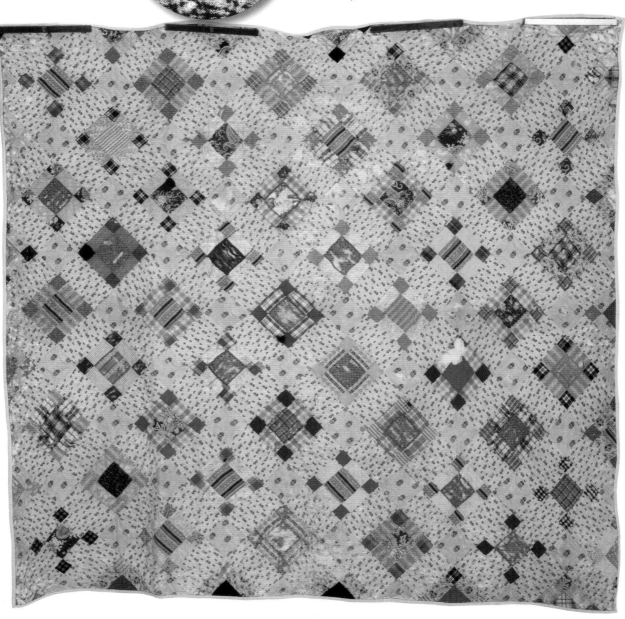

Minnesota State Fair Quilts

The first Minnesota fair, held in 1854, was a territorial fair, as Minnesota was not yet a state. Items exhibited that year were mostly vegetables and agricultural animals; at that time there was no women's building. While researching for the book *Blue Ribbon: A Social and Pictorial History of the Minnesota State Fair*, Karal Ann Marling found this statement about the first Minnesota fair:

> *James S. Hough remembers that first year. There was no Women's Building either, of course, since there were only about fifty ladies resident in the district, few of whom had the time to do the fancywork traditionally displayed by wives and daughters at agricultural shows back East. But there was a sewing machine up on the second floor. A clumsy affair, it was still "the first one seen here" and quickly gathered a crowd that gawked at "the mystic needle as it rapidly put stitch after stitch in a piece of cloth."[18]*

A few years later at the 1857 Minnesota fair, the premium book lists a division for Best Patchwork Quilt with a premium of three dollars.[19] There was no fair in 1858 because of the poor economy. In 1859, the Fourth Union Fair was presented by Hennepin County and the Territorial Agricultural Organization. It was the first since Minnesota had reached statehood. The fair took place on a fifteen-acre site at the corner of Marquette Avenue and Fifth Street in Minneapolis. That year there was a women's exhibit.[20]

NINE PATCH

Marie Morrissette was born in 1847 in the Little Canada settlement north of St. Paul. She was twelve years old when she entered this quilt at the 1859 Minnesota fair. The quilt is a variation of a Nine Patch with alternating rectangular blocks of a light print fabric. Marie chose various prints in pink, blue, and cream colors. The backing is an all-over floral print, and many fabrics are repeated throughout the quilt. The Minnesota History Center information from the maker's grandson and donor of the quilt, Elvert Connelly, states that this quilt won first prize at the 1859 fair. Marie was married to Alphonse Farrell in 1870 and lived in the St. Paul area all her life. Her obituary states, "A woman, who saw a city of 271,000 grow up from the raw wilderness in her 84-year span of life, died here Sunday."[21] She saw and participated in the beginnings of the Minnesota State Fair and watched as the state of Minnesota evolved. The family knows of no other quilts made by Marie.

Fairs played an important part in drawing immigrants to the state. Fairs were well known in the East and a state that had an organized agricultural society fair was considered "civilized." Exhibiting agricultural products was a way to promote a state's resources. Some thought that the development of a Minnesota fair would help dispel rumors that Minnesota was a frozen land. With an increase in fair participants, the women's areas expanded and more classes were added for quiltmakers. In 1860, three premium classes were listed for quilts: White Quilt, Patchwork, and Silk Quilt.[22] For a number of years, the fair traveled from site to site, but in 1885 the fair moved to the Hamline area and permanent buildings were erected. The railroad ran along the southern edge of the grounds, bringing supplies and fairgoers to the fair. Exhibitors competed in many more divisions than the fair goers of earlier times. The grounds had grown, and the entries were exceptional examples of individual work. Nearly a century after Marie Morissette entered her quilt in the Minnesota fair, the next quilt continued the tradition.

CALICO ROSE QUILT

In 1950, Boletta Lund Huntington's Calico Rose quilt won first premium at the Stearns County Fair in the appliqué quilt class before going on to win a first premium sweepstakes at the state fair. At the state fair, judges evaluated quilts in several different areas.

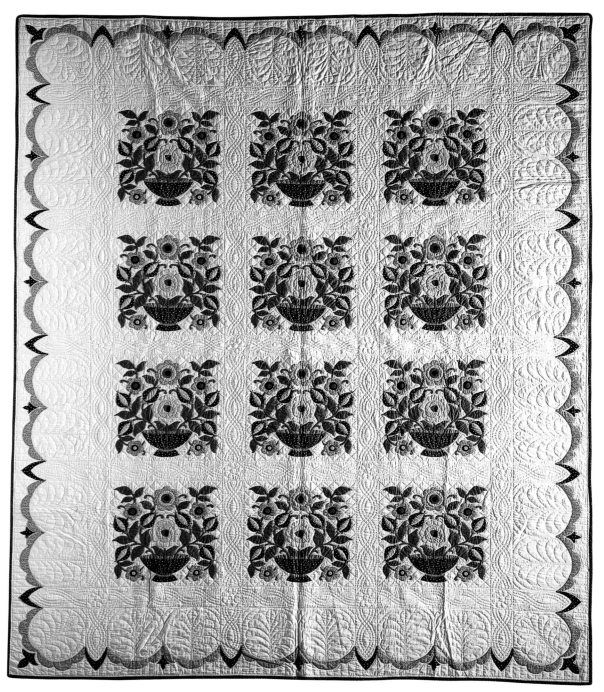

Calico Rose | Date: circa 1950 | Maker: Boletta Lund Huntington | Size: 83½" x 99" | Owner: Private collection

This Calico Rose quilt won an honorary mention at the Minnesota State Fair.

MINNESOTA STATE FAIR
Score Card
NEEDLECRAFT

Lot No. G-147   Entry 1a 6 9

			SCORE
I. General Appearance			
Beauty and Character		10	10
Uninteresting	Distinctive		
Weak	Strong		
Disturbing	Satisfying		
Outmoded	Stylish		
Color		10	9
Too bright or too dull	Pleasing		
Poor combination	Harmonious		
Design—Structural and decorative		20	17
Unsuited to use	Suited to use		
Unsuited to material	Suited to material		
Unsuited to technique	Suited to technique		
Unrelated to structure	Structurally good		
Naturalistic	Appropriate		
Confused, overdone	Simple, dignified		
Condition of article		10	10
Worn or faded	New-looking		
Soiled	Clean		
Wrinkled or untidy	Well pressed or neat		
II. Materials used		20	20
Poor quality	Good quality		
Inappropriate	Well adapted to use		
Unsuited to technique	Suited to processes used		
III. Workmanship		30	30
Perfection of process used			
Choice and handling of finishes			
Other remarks			
		100	C

Remarks.............

Signature of Judge.....F. K. Zartner. C.....

Signature of Clerk.....H. H.....

Score card for the Calico Rose quilt

Quiltmaker Boletta Huntington with her Calico Rose Quilt appeared in the St. Paul Pioneer Press.

Boletta Huntington made the Calico Rose Quilt from a purchased kit, Paragon Kit #1082, over a five-year period. Kits contained the patterns and the supplies needed to make a quilt top, and were available from the 1920s through the 1980s. This appliqué quilt consists of twelve blocks in two shades of pink, featuring roses and rose buds in a dark vase. The blocks are sewn together with a sashing of cream cotton fabric. A cream border surrounded by an appliqué swag border frames this quilt. It is an excellent example of a well-made kit quilt. Boletta completed the intricate appliqué in overcast stitches. The quilt is handquilted with even stitches in cable and fan designs.

Boletta was born in 1890 and was an art student at the University of Minnesota from 1909 until 1912. She lived in the Paynesville area and enjoyed many hobbies over the years. According to her family, her favorite and most time-consuming hobby was making quilts. She was a faithful member of the Martha Circle quilting group of Grace United Methodist Church in Paynesville. Her family estimates that Boletta made more than fifty quilts between 1930 and 1960.

A photo of Boletta and her quilt appeared in the *Saint Paul Pioneer Press* in August 1952. The reporter stated, "A visit to the home activities department of the State Fair, where more than 150 quilts are displayed, leaves no doubt that the North Star state excels in quilt champions. The block-long show cases are filled with prize-winners, and here are all the well-known patterns, beloved of every woman who knows her quilts."[23] Each year the Minnesota State Fair exhibits quilts, continuing the connection of quilters to the greater community by displaying their beautiful workmanship.

Chapter Four

Connections to Economics

BY JEAN CARLTON

Virtually all aspects of quiltmaking, including the style or design of the quilt, the fabrics used, or the techniques employed, are profoundly influenced by economic conditions at the time the quilt is made. Economic conditions also directly affect the availability of quilting supplies and the time one has to spend making a quilt. Until American textile mills were established, all fabric had to be imported, usually from England or France, making it a scarce and very expensive commodity. By 1850, when American textile mills were in full production and a wide variety of fabrics were available at a reasonable cost, quiltmaking became very popular among women of all economic classes.

Other events such as war, economic depression, and the Industrial Revolution had an impact on the American economy, and in turn affected quiltmaking. During wartime, especially the Civil War and World War I, textile mills filled orders for troops first, resulting in a scarcity of fabrics for home use. Leisure time was also less available, as pitching in to help with the war effort became the patriotic thing to do. The many small sewing groups and ladies aid societies already in place for charitable work were now organized specifically for relief efforts. Setting up days to work together, as well as working at home individually, women made huge contributions to the war efforts. Women rolled bandages and made much-needed bedding and clothing. One relief effort in Boston produced five thousand shirts in five days![1]

The Great Depression of 1929, probably the most devastating economic event in our nation's history, had a different affect on quiltmaking than one might imagine. Quiltmaking actually flourished, despite the shortage of fabric and money. Women were inspired to find ways to make do with what they had, affecting the styles but not reducing the quantity of quilts produced. As part of the Chicago World's Fair of 1933, Sears Roebuck & Company announced a national quilt competition with prize money for the winners. Quilters across the country submitted more than twenty-four thousand quilts by the deadline less than six months later![2]

During World War II, many women took factory jobs to fill the worker shortages left by the men. When the war ended, many continued to work outside the home, leaving them less leisure time for quilting. Postwar prosperity made commercial goods widely available and homemade items were scorned by many as old-fashioned. Though all quilts reflect the times in which they were made, fundraising quilts were created specifically to raise money, and utility and Depression-era quilts exemplify the "waste not, want not" mentality by maximizing use of available materials and time in their creation.

WAGON WHEEL QUILT

This striking red and white signature quilt is composed of solid red "wheels" appliquéd on white background squares. A flannel blanket serves as batting and yarn ties hold the layers together. The spaces between the spokes and the centers contain 274 signatures. Rose Schrader Edsill assembled the blocks.

Fundraising Quilts

Groups of women volunteers have long used their domestic skills to contribute to the good of their community. Great numbers of independent ladies aid societies, relief societies, sewing circles, and soldiers aid societies formed to meet specific needs. Quilts provided a way for women to raise money to support their beliefs, including abolition, prohibition, and suffrage; to help in war efforts, as when making Red Cross quilts; or contribute to local needs.

By 1863, the United States Sanitary Commission, whose purpose was to provide supplies and medical care for the Union soldiers, helped consolidate these independent efforts with huge fairs. Women were the heart of this effort, having had the experience of successfully organizing their smaller sewing societies.

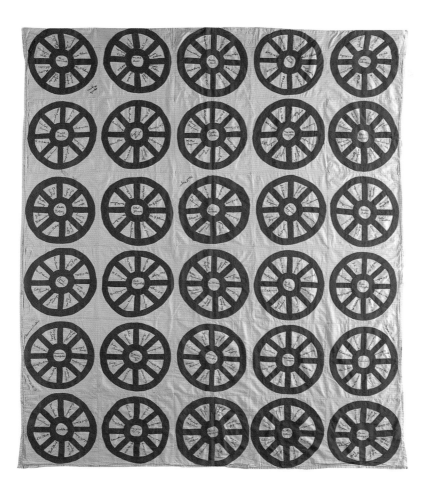

**Wagon Wheel | DATE: 1914–1915
MAKER: Ladies Aid Society of
Cazenovia, Minnesota | SIZE: 70"
x 85" | OWNER: Maxine Reynolds
Tonsfeldt**

*The open areas between the "spokes"
on this Wagon Wheel fundraising quilt
provided an ideal space for the many
signatures collected.*

These fairs, which were held over several days, raised money by providing entertainment or selling garden produce, handcrafted furniture, needlework, knitted afghans, and quilts. The fairs were so successful that President Abraham Lincoln praised the women who organized them, recognizing their important role in relieving the suffering of soldiers and their families.[3]

At the beginning of the twentieth century, women from church or town sewing circles quickly organized to meet the needs of the community. Embroidered signature quilts became a popular way to raise funds for such things as a new floor or furnace for a public building, an addition or other improvement to a church, or even road repair. A donation, typically ten cents, bought the right to have one's name included on the quilt. In some cases, having a name added to a special area of the quilt, such as the center, required a higher donation. Sometimes the donor actually signed the fabric block. More often the woman collecting the money would write names on her block, or the group would select one person to pen the names before the embroidery began. There may have been some healthy competition between the women as they tried to obtain the most donations or raced to complete their blocks before the others. The group most likely organized a sewing day to assemble the blocks and then gathered together to quilt the completed top. The community church, town hall, or one of the lady's homes typically served as place to meet and work.

The finished quilts were often auctioned or raffled off, although some communities avoided raffles because they were likened to gambling. Sometimes the winner would donate the quilt back to the organization, allowing the group to earn more money in a second raffle. If the bids were too low and one of the women who helped make the quilt had grown especially attached to it, she might make the winning bid. Charitable women gave their time and talents to make these quilts, but as Jane Kolter observes in *Forget Me Not: A Gallery of Friendship and Album Quilts*, "Help-

Red Embroidered Quilt
DATE: **1910** | MAKER:
Ladies of the Christ
Evangelical Church of
Olivia, Minnesota
SIZE: **72" x 80"**
OWNER: **Collection**
of Renville County
Historical Society and
Museum

The pastor of the church,
who had beautiful
handwriting, was asked
to write the names on the
quilt before the ladies
began their embroidery.

ing others has often been women's work and men's money." [4] Often the buyer was the husband of one of the makers or another man in town. Men bought the Red Embroidered quilt and the Appliqué Rose quilt included in this chapter.

Twenty quilts with fundraising connections were documented in Minnesota. The earliest dated 1851 and the latest 1950; more than half were made in the first quarter of the twentieth century. Organized groups such as the Dorcas Society of Ebenezer Lutheran Church in North Dakota or the Ladies of Christ Evangelical Church in Olivia, Minnesota, made many of the quilts. Red and white was a popular color combination, probably because of the known fastness of red dye at the time.

The practice of raising money through quiltmaking is still going strong in Minnesota. Every year the

state quilt guild, Minnesota Quilters, creates a quilt to be raffled off at the annual show in June. Many smaller quilt groups and guilds throughout the state do the same at their individual shows. Guilds designate monies for a variety of causes, often funding for future shows, expanding the guild library, or hiring quilt teachers for educational programs. Now, as in the past, this activity brings quilters together, combining fellowship with productivity.

RED EMBROIDERED QUILT

Quilting a "petal" around each embroidered name created a flower motif that enhanced the graphic appeal of this quilt. Each member of the group was responsible for one block, placing her name in the middle and collecting ten cents for each signature on her block. The ladies asked the pastor of the church, who had beautiful handwriting, to write all the names. The ladies then embroidered with red thread in an outline stitch. Henry Fehr, Sr. won the quilt at auction with a bid of $105, the equivalent of $1,947 in today's dollars![5]

THE TENNEY QUILT

In 1928, the town of Tenney in the Red River Valley of northwestern Minnesota had a population of only 150, yet this quilt contains more than 700 names! How could so many names have been gathered? Some names appear more than once, and the names of several fictional and literary characters such as Old King Cole, Mother Goose, and Rip Van Winkle were added also. Everyone got into the spirit of the fun with high school girls contributing their dime and a silly name. The enthusiasm is understandable, as any funds raised would go toward a much-needed furnace in the town hall—which also served as the dance hall. It boasted a hardwood dance floor and a stage with ornate velvet curtains. It became Tenney's claim to fame when Lawrence Welk and his orchestra came to town.

The Larson General Store purchased an entire block for two dollars, a rate presumably set by figuring that twenty names could have been sold for a place on that block. The Larson block was placed toward the center of the quilt, appropriately reflecting the store's central role in the town.

The winner of the quilt at auction was LaVanche Solvie Gill, a relative of the Larson family. She later passed it on to her niece, Helen Jo Larson Leaf, the daughter of the owner of the Larson General Store and mother of its current owner, keeping this special quilt in the family.

Today, large corporate farms have bought up the land around Tenney, and most of the homes have been razed. The 2000 census recorded six residents. Fortunately, this quilt remains to document the spirit of a lively Minnesota prairie town during the early years of the twentieth century.

The small town of Tenney got into the spirit of fundraising as they contributed ten cents in the name of such fictional characters as Scrooge, Pollyanna, Rip Van Winkle, and Lady Macbeth.

**Signature Quilt | DATE: 1928
MAKERS: Tenney town ladies
SIZE: 73" x 86" | OWNER: Heidi Haagenson**

More than 700 signatures were included on this fundraising quilt, made in a town of only 150 residents.

APPLIQUÉ ROSE QUILT

This traditional quilt of pieced baskets with appliquéd flowers demonstrates that not all quilts made to raise money contained signatures or names. We know it was auctioned by the Ebenezer Lutheran Church in Northwood, North Dakota, in the 1940s and that Knut E. Thorsgard, the father of the current owner, had the winning bid. Unfortunately, there is no information about what the funds were used for. Knut passed the quilt along to his daughter, a Minnesota resident, in 1976.

Utility Quilts

Utility quilts best portray the attitude of thrift and practicality in quiltmaking. Out of necessity, quiltmakers sewed together any and all available textiles to pro-

vide warmth. Most likely, the earliest quilts were made for everyday use. Because these quilts were often used until they fell apart, there is no doubt that many more were made than we will ever know. Utility quilts were not put away "for good" or taken out only on Sunday like the fancy quilts made as show pieces to demonstrate the maker's needlework skills.

The objective of these quilts is a practical one—to get warm covers on the bed and to do so quickly. To this end, the overall design is often simple, incorporating larger pieces of sturdy fabrics, leftover clothing, remnants from other sewing projects, or even salesmen's samples. The quilt, sometimes referred to as a comfort or comforter, is often tied with string or yarn for a quick finish. In those that are quilted, the maker may use heavier thread and more primitive stiching in a simple

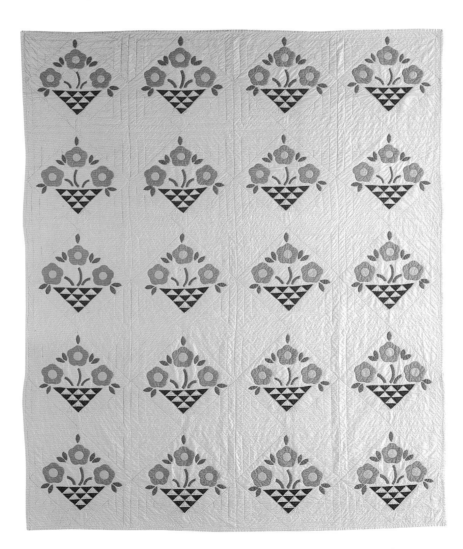

Appliqué Rose | DATE: 1940
MAKERS: Dorcas Society of
Ebenezer Lutheran Church
of Northwood, North Dakota
SIZE: 77" x 99" | OWNER:
Kathryn Erickson

Not all fundraising quilts contain signatures.

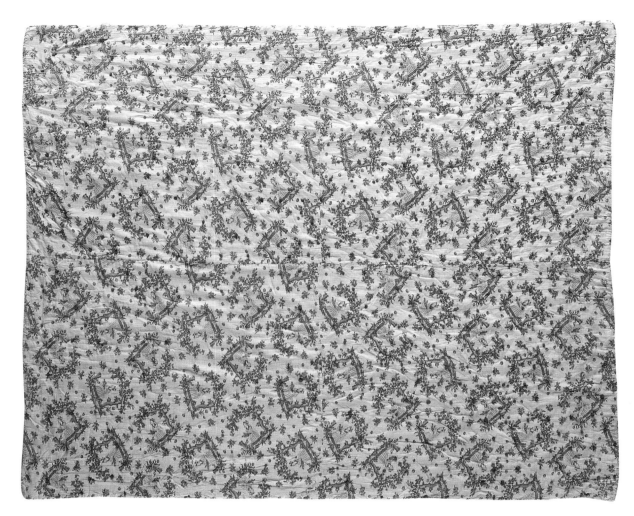

Wholecloth | DATE: **c. 1930** | MAKER: **Luella Clauson Peterson** | SIZE: **71" x 85"** | OWNER: **Candyce Jutila, granddaughter of maker**

Four whole feed sacks were sewn together to make this simple but functional utility quilt.

grid, overall design, or near the seam line. Most of these quilts do not have borders, possibly because they would require too much fabric. The batting may be an old blanket or even another quilt too worn to be serviceable anymore.[6] Old clothing, curtains, or even paper may be used as filler. The backing may also be pieced.

One might assume that more quilts of this type were produced in areas of poverty and/or during economic depression, but people of all classes needed usable, sturdy quilts. Serviceable quilts were made for hired hands and used in cowboy's bedrolls (called soogans). Even today's quilters, often with ample resources, employ the same techniques and philosophy when they make picnic quilts or quilts to send off with college students.

The quilts featured in this chapter demonstrate that quiltmakers can be quite creative in their use of the materials they have on hand.

WHOLECLOTH QUILT

This feed sack wholecloth quilt represents the ultimate in thrift of both materials and time. Luella Clauson Peterson, who spent most of her life in Pelican Rapids, Minnesota, sewed together four printed sacks of the same design and then tied the layers together with wool and yarn. There is no binding. Instead, the edges of both the top and the backing are turned in and stitched in what is referred to as a knife edge finish, an easy and economical method requiring no extra fabric.

In addition to the many quilts she made for family members, Agnes Grundvald made rugs, clothing, and soap.

Rail Fence variations | DATE: c. 1965 | MAKER: Agnes Grundvald (1900–1981) | SIZE: 72" x 77" and 68" x 79" | OWNER: Jean Carlton, niece of maker

A quiltmaker often develops a fondness for one or two favorite designs.

RAIL FENCE QUILTS

Agnes Grundvald made this pair of Rail Fence quilts, each shown folded in half. Agnes, the first of seven children, was born in 1900 on a farm in Pope County, Minnesota. She began sewing at a young age. One of her earliest quilts was made from the men's old work pants, and the family used it in the horse-drawn buggy during trips to town. When her mother saw it, she thought it was so nice that she wanted to take it into the house. Agnes eventually moved to "The Cities" (Minneapolis and St. Paul), where she made many quilts for her relatives from the multitude of scraps she received from people who knew she was a quiltmaker. If she bought yardage, it was usually for the backings. The pine-paneled workroom in her basement was a riot of color, with piles of fabric scraps strewn all about. It is not uncommon for a quiltmaker to develop a fondness for one or two favorite designs, and Agnes loved making Rail Fence and Log Cabin quilts. When

she wasn't quilting, she braided wool rugs from used clothing, crocheted rugs from cotton strips, sewed clothing, knit, gardened, and made her own lye soap. She was known for saying, "I don't see how anyone could be bored."

Each of these utility quilts makes use of larger pieces of leftovers from garment sewing. The darker quilt, pictured on the bottom, is made of a heavier cotton fabric called tarpoon, popular for skirts, pants, and jackets in the 1960s. The quilt is backed with a heavy green twill and bound with scraps of the plaids pieced together.

The quilt on the top is made entirely of corduroy, giving it an especially lustrous vibrancy. A cotton calico print of yellow flowers on a blue background forms the quilt's backing, and a knife-edge finish eliminates the need for binding. Neither quilt has a border. Both are handquilted rather primitively with a heavy cotton thread along the seam lines. The thoughtful placement of solids and use of color in these quilts demonstrate a commonality in utility quilts: function and beauty can coexist.

TRIP AROUND THE WORLD QUILT

Any quilt that incorporates clothing of a family member takes on special meaning. Anna Viglesdotter Jondal used wool rectangles cut from the suits of the men in the John Jondal family to make this Trip Around the World variation. Anna was born in Norway and immigrated to the United States in 1885 with her husband John Knute Gundvedt. John was a fisherman on the North Sea, and the couple came to America to escape the dangers of his job, bringing their three children with them. One, a little girl of two, was buried at sea during the journey. When the family arrived in New York, they changed their last name to Jondal, in honor of their village on the Hardangar Fjord in Norway. They made their way to Hayfield, Minnesota, where they farmed the land and eventually raised eleven children.

Anna loved handwork. She crocheted, did Hardanger embroidery, hooked rugs, and even wove fabric on a loom in the garage during the summer months. She epitomized the thrifty mindset, unraveling old sweaters to knit mittens for her grandchildren after first tracing their hands on paper.

Anna's Trip Around the World quilt is a bit unusual. Although the pattern of the patches begins in a Trip Around the World arrangement, the traveler seems to wander off course, the pattern becoming less defined toward the corners. This may have been a design choice, but is more likely a result of working within the limitations of available fabrics. Anna used a cotton blanket as batting and tied the quilt layers together at the intersections with wool yarn.

Anna epitomized the thrifty mindset, unraveling old sweaters to knit mittens for her grandchildren.

Trip Around the World variation
DATE: **c. 1915** | MAKER: **Anna Viglesdotter Jondal (1857–1939)** | SIZE: **66" x 76"** | OWNER: **Joan Anderson**

Wool from men's suits was used to make this Trip Around the World variation.

In 1884, Louise Englemann Shaeffer was married in a black dress and white veil, which, according to German tradition, brought good luck. Her family reports that the wedding dress was later "made over" into a Sunday dress. Her family believes that pieces of it can be found in this quilt. Louise often pinned notes to various household items, a habit that her descendants now appreciate because of the valuable historical information the notes convey. Pinned to this quilt was a small piece of paper marked, "1905." Louise finished the edge by bringing the yellow and green plaid backing to the front. The quilt's bold geometry, along with the added design element created with the four strand ties, make this utility quilt of wools and velvets a work of art, even though it was made to be used every day by a farm family enduring the cold winters of the Minnesota prairie. This quilt was displayed in "Q" is for Quilts," part of the "Minnesota: A to Z" exhibit at the Minnesota Historical Society.

Depression-Era Quilts

The Great Depression of 1929 affected the entire nation, but the largely rural state of Minnesota, where farmers were used to being self-sufficient, may have had a slight advantage. Farmers could grow their own food, and many had chickens in the yard as well as cattle or pigs.

Family members believe some of the black wool used to make Louise's wedding dress in 1884 was used in this quilt.

Rob Peter to Pay Paul variation | DATE: 1905 | MAKER: Louise Englemann Shaeffer (1863–1914) | SIZE: 77" x 84" | OWNER: Mary Louise Sanders, granddaughter of maker

Louise would probably have been shocked to see her humble quilt on exhibit in the Minnesota Historical Society since, according to her granddaughter, she didn't "make a fuss" about the work she did—everyone worked and did what needed doing. (Courtesy of the Minnesota Historical Society)

Tulips | DATE: c. 1935
MAKER: **Zelda Fredericka Dora Graplar Detert (b. 1912)**
SIZE: 90" x 90" | OWNER:
Zelda Fredericka Dora Graplar Detert

Zelda made this quilt using only a picture from a magazine for a pattern.

In spite of the shortage of goods, quiltmaking experienced a resurgence during the Depression, as the time-honored values of thrift and productivity were brought to the forefront. Quilt patterns that made use of very small pieces, such as Grandmother's Flower Garden and Double Wedding Ring, became popular because small bits of fabric from other sewing projects or unworn pieces of old clothing were easy to come by. Nothing was wasted. The printed cloth sacks used to package flour, sugar, and chicken feed were recycled for home decorating and clothing for the family. A farm woman with chickens had a lot of "free" fabric in the sacks once the feed was gone. The most common one-hundred-pound sack provided more than a yard of fabric. Women sometimes went along on the trip to the feed store to ensure they'd have enough sacks of the same print to make curtains or pajamas. Even the string removed from the sack was saved for a variety of uses. The thriftiest women carefully removed basting thread and rewound it for the next project!

Many commercial quilt patterns were published at this time in newspapers and farm journals. Though it may have only cost ten cents to send for the pattern, money was scarce, and many quiltmakers created their own patterns by studying the drawings. Kits containing a pattern and all necessary fabric were widely available. Most of the quilts made during this especially bleak time for our nation are bright and cheerful, reflecting the desire to look on the bright side and furnish a home as a pleasant retreat from the outside world.

TULIP QUILT

Zelda Detert pieced, handappliquéd, and embroidered this Tulip Quilt, making her own pattern from a picture of a similar quilt she saw in *Farmer* magazine. She completed the quilting in lavender perle cotton in a one-inch diagonal grid with help from Ida Grapler and Wilma Anderson, Zelda's mother and sister. She tells of often gathering with neighbors to help each other finish quilts. She also remembers participating in the tradition of bouncing a cat in the middle of the completed quilt; whichever girl the cat jumped nearest as it escaped the silliness would be the next to be married!

Mildred and Herbert Freuchte

Flower Garden | DATE: 1932–1933 | MAKER: Mildred Weber Fruechte (b. 1914) | SIZE: 63" x 80" | OWNER: Carolyn Fruechte

Mildred and Herbert Freuchte both worked on their "honeymoon" quilt. Mildred embroidered flowers from a kit she purchased before she was married. This was the first and only quilt she ever made.

HONEYMOON QUILT

In preparation for her upcoming marriage, Mildred Fruechte began embroidering pre-stamped floral designs from a state-flowers kit she had purchased. It is very similar to a design in Ruby McKim's *101 Patchwork Patterns*, first published in 1931. Mildred assembled the blocks and picket-fence border entirely by hand. She called it her honeymoon quilt, because she and her husband Herbert completed it together during the long winter evenings of their first year of marriage. She says she can still tell which stitches he put in—they're just a bit longer than hers! It is a very special family quilt, as it is the only quilt Mildred ever made. She enjoyed knitting, crocheting, and other needlework.

SPOOLS QUILT

This Spools quilt was made in Indiana and came to Minnesota with Lea MacDonald, the granddaughter of the maker. Lea used to hide under her "Mamaw's" quilt frame to avoid having to go home after a visit. Quiltmaker Myrtle Lemmons Freshley had a reputation as a great seamstress. When her husband died quite young, she spent her days sewing for hire to provide for her family. In the evenings, she relaxed by hooking rugs or quilting at the frame set up in her bedroom. Over the years she made many quilts, never selling them but giving them to family members or using them herself.

The fabrics in this quilt are believed to be feed sacks collected during World War II. Her careful fabric placement creates an interesting diagonal graphic.

Spools | c. 1940 | MAKER: Myrtle (Mamaw) Lemmons Freshley | SIZE: 70" x 80" | OWNER: Private collection

In this Spools quilt, diagonal bands of color result from thoughtful fabric placement.

Gertrude Ahmann, a fine seamstress and quiltmaker, used her treadle sewing machine until 1978.

Turkey Tracks | Date: 1936 | Maker: Gertrude Ahmann (1889–1986)
Size: 76" x 95" | Owner: Rosemary Walz

As a farm wife, Gertrude had easy access to feed sack fabrics for her Turkey Tracks quilt.

Turkey Tracks Quilt

Gertrude Buermann was born in Germany in 1889 and came to Richmond, Minnesota, with her family at the turn of the century. She learned how to sew at the age of seven. When she was about ten years old, her father brought home a sewing machine and told her, "You are the seamstress now." She taught herself to use a sewing machine and made dresses for herself and her sister. Gertrude married Henry Ahmann in 1936. The couple lived on a farm where they raised chickens and cows as well as nine children. They had no electricity for many years and yet somehow Gertrude made more than two hundred quilts, as well clothing for the family! Her daughter, Rosemary, recalls the year 1945. She was in high school and had never had a "boughten" dress. She saw one in a shop window that she loved, but her mother said it was too expensive. One day when Rosemary came home from school, her mother surprised her with a completed dress, just like the one she'd admired. Gertrude had copied the dress exactly without following a pattern.

Gertrude was still sewing in her nineties; she used her treadle machine until 1978 when she got an elec-

tric machine with a zigzag stitch. One day Rosemary arrived home to find her mother busy sewing miscellaneous odds and ends together in a haphazard arrangement. She looked up with a smile and said, "This is a CRAAAAAZY quilt!"

Gertrude gave many quilts to each of her children, grandchildren, nieces, nephews, and great-grandchildren. She also enjoyed knitting, embroidery, and other handwork. She exemplifies the thrifty homemaker in rural Minnesota, making good use of time and materials.

Gertrude's Turkey Tracks quilt includes many of the typical feed sack prints that would have been readily available to her as a farm wife. It is handquilted in rows less than one inch apart with a daisy design in the plain-setting blocks. To ensure that the owner washed the quilt correctly, she often noted the type of filler she used. Embroidered on the back of this quilt is the word "blanket."

Pink Strippy Quilt

This quilt is one of approximately fifty quilts that Katherine Stromberg made. It must have been a published pattern, as there is one just like it pictured in *The Romance of the Patchwork Quilt in America* by Carrie Hall and Rose Kretsinger. Katherine was a very conscientious quilter. She had quilting parties but was known to undo poorly done stitches after her guests left! She used bits of flour-sack prints for the appliquéd flowers, which she set in vertical columns, alternating with solid pink cotton.

"Strippy" | **DATE: c. 1945** | **MAKER: Katherine Hollensfeld Stromberg (1908–1979)** | **SIZE: 79" x 92"** | **OWNERS: Lulubeth and Marvin Stromberg**

This "strippy"-style floral appliqué quilt design has been seen in several publications, indicating that it was a commercially published pattern.

Printed Feed Sacks

Printed feed and flour sacks became common in the 1930s and 1940s, but fabric sacks have been used since the early 1800s as containers for a wide variety of commodities. Those early sacks were typically made of plain woven cotton, often printed with name or product information that was difficult to remove. Resourceful women of the time devised methods to remove the lettering and found a variety of uses for the sacks.

As the twentieth century progressed, the manufacturers of products such as flour, sugar, feed, and seed saw a way to increase sales by attracting the interest of American housewives. The profusion of pretty prints and solids in bright pastel tones that we associate with the term "feed sack" today were the result of this competitive strategy. The use (or, more appropriately, re-use) of these sacks was promoted in home economics classes, by patterns printed with yardage requirements given in number of sacks, and with traveling style shows featuring the many items that could be made from the sacks. The industry used terms such as "dress good bags," "fashion or glamour sacks," and "pretties" to promote garment sewing and elevate the status of the feed sacks in the eyes of women from all economic classes. It has been estimated that more than fifty million "dress goods" bags had been manufactured by 1940. The term "feed sack" is a slight misnomer, as more than 40 percent of the printed bags were used to package flour. "Sack and Snack Clubs" became a popular way to socialize and swap sacks.[8]

The green and white checked bag is stamped "General Mills."

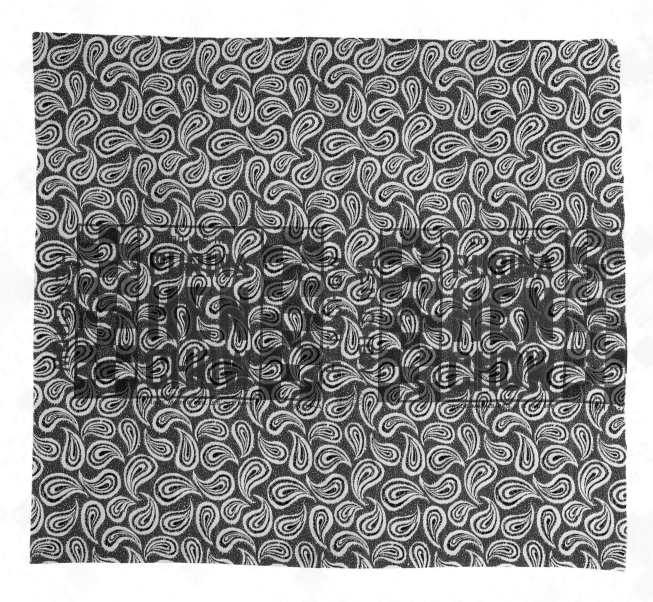

The words "Purina Hen Chow" were printed directly onto the paisley fabric of this feedsack.

The Bemis Bag Company, headquartered in Minneapolis, became one of the largest bag makers in the world, with fifteen bag manufacturing plants and four textile mills. Some manufacturers resisted the printed bag, as it obscured the name of the company and its product. In the 1940s, Bemis introduced and later patented a paper label that was attached to the bag with a water-soluble paste. This label guaranteed brand identity while allowing easy removal.

Though some printed bags are still made today, the popularity of dress goods sacks reached their peak in the mid 1940s, when the triple-walled paper sack, costing about one-third of the price of the equivalent-size cotton sack, became the most economical packaging choice. The feed sacks survive today in a plethora of garments, household items, and quilts as testaments to the thriftiness of American housewives and to very savvy marketing campaigns!

Chapter Five

Connections to Traditional Quiltmaking

BY LINDA NORTHWAY KOSFELD

From the mid 1800s until early in the twentieth century, settlers brought quilts to Minnesota from many other states and countries. The families who were already settled in Minnesota relied on each new group of immigrants to inform them about the latest fashions and trends from back east. People were eager to drop in to welcome new neighbors and see what they had brought with them.

Women were especially interested to see the new neighbors' furnishings, including the quilts. Seeing new quilts and copying them was one way that quilters in Minnesota learned about different quilt blocks and patterns, since quilt patterns were not printed with any frequency until after 1900. In the 1890s, Sears Roebuck and Montgomery Ward offered quilt patterns for a dime with the purchase of yard goods from their respective catalogs.

Quilters also shared patterns through letters. A relative or friend might send a scrap of fabric from a quilt she was making and include a sketch of the block she was using. This scrap of fabric and the block pattern was a means of staying connected to family and friends who were many miles away. Some of these shared patterns became traditional patterns—patterns that quilters enjoy making and that remain popular,

regardless of the decade or century. Irish Chain, Log Cabin, Hexagon, Fan, Double Wedding Ring, Crazy, and any of the Star patterns can be made in designs and color combinations to reflect a quiltmaker's own style. Traditional quilt patterns are perfect for using scraps of fabric. For early quilters, this meant saving money and avoiding the long wait for a catalog order or the next trip to town.

Sampler Quilts

Quilters often made Sampler quilts with the blocks they accumulated when they copied new patterns. The quilter would make a block and then add this new pattern to her sewing basket. That way, she would have the pattern if she ever wanted to use the block in a quilt. After accumulating a number of these single blocks, the quiltmaker might decide to use all of them in one quilt, so they would not be wasted.

In another type of sampler quilt, each block is a different design, but they have a planned, related color scheme. Beginning quilters often make such samplers as a way to practice different techniques. Appliquéd quilts can also be done in the sampler style, with each block in a different design.

A close look at Hazel's exceptional appliqué work

**Sampler quilt, Baltimore Album style | DATE: 1974
MAKER: Hazel Simpson Morehouse | SIZE: 85" x 85"
OWNERS: Irene Ensrud and Mildred Morehouse, the
maker's daughters**

Hazel patiently acquired just the right red and green fabrics before starting her quilt.

BALTIMORE ALBUM STYLE SAMPLER

There were very few Sampler quilts documented in Minnesota. This one was made by Hazel Simpson Morehouse in Montevideo. It was made in the style of a Baltimore Album, using red and green fabrics on a white background. According to Hazel's family, she acquired the pattern from a magazine, probably *The Farm Journal*, in 1922 or 1923. Hazel did not make the quilt until 1974, however, after she had acquired all of the small red and green prints. She believed that quilting should be enjoyed and not hurried. The appliqué work in the quilt is excellent—and definitely not hurried.

There are a few interesting twists to this quilt's story. When the quilt was photographed, observers noticed that some faint blue marks were visible on the blocks. It looked as if the blocks may have come pre-marked, possibly from a magazine mail-order ad. Another interesting discovery was that, in 2000, Chitra Publications published block patterns for a quilt almost identical to this one in their book *Grandma's Last Quilt: Traditional and Original Appliqué Designs* by Blanche Burkett White. The exact origin of that quilt's pattern is unknown.

Hexagon Quilts

Hexagon quilts have been popular in this country throughout its quilting history, with examples dating from the early 1800s. The British have a long history with this pattern, and English settlers may have influenced its popularity in America.

The name "Hexagon" describes the six-sided block itself. A Hexagon quilt is known as a single-patch quilt, meaning that all of the pieces are one shape. The earliest patterns using the hexagon shape were named Mosaic or Honeycomb. At the end of the nineteenth century, quilters began to refer to this pattern as Grandmother's Garden or Grandmother's Flower Garden. It was one of the most frequently made patterns in the early twentieth century and continues to be popular today. The Minnesota Quilt Project discovered 228 Hexagon quilts out of a total of 3,736 documented quilts, reflecting Minnesota's connection to the mainstream influences of quilting.

In April 1850, *Godey's Lady's Book*, a popular women's periodical at the time, published an illustration of single block patterns, including hexagons with both equal and unequal sides. The instructions read:

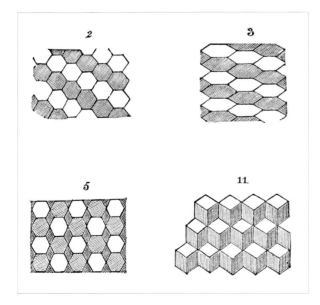

Patchwork illustrations from Godey's Lady's Book, *April 1850.*

"The material necessary for patchwork are such portions of wearing apparel. . . . as would otherwise be thrown away, or saved for the rag-man. The next necessary article is some stiff paper, to form the shapes, and lastly the design-shapes, cut out in tin and the designs themselves. The materials should be arranged into shades and qualities. . . . The pattern should be placed before the person, and the shades being selected, the several pieces arranged so as to form the design, and the edges then neatly sewn together; after which they are either pressed or ironed, the papers removed, and the lining proceeded with." [1]

MOSAIC HEXAGON QUILT

The instructions from *Godey's Lady's Book* would certainly fit this quilt purchased at a farm auction near Atwater, Minnesota. No information about the quilter is available, but the complexity of her design and use of color speak of a talented and patient piecer. Each of the hexagons is only three-quarters of an inch on each side. Each hexagon was pieced in the English style over paper and handstitched together. Fabrics include silk, velvet, satin, brocade, and grosgrain in prints, dots, check, stripes, and solids. The back is plain brown cotton. An unusual feature is the three-inch upholstery fabric with attached fringe that serves as the outside border. Although there is deterioration in the silk fabrics, it is an exciting example of the artistic possibilities of the Hexagon pattern. *Godey's* instruction to remove the papers was disregarded by this quilter, and they remain in the quilt.

Hexagon (Mosaic) | DATE: c. 1880 | MAKER: Unknown SIZE: 78" x 91" including fringe | OWNER: Judy Sheehan

Painstaking English paper piecing *by an unknown quilter resulted in an artistic, colorful design.*

Honeycomb | Date: **c. 1900** | Maker: **Ingeborg Charlotte Stromberg (1870–1962)** | Size: **69" x 92"** Owner: **Carolyn Abbott**

Members of Ingeborg's family said that "she was the only one in the family impractical enough to make a quilt from silk."

Left: Quiltmaker Ingeborg Stromberg

Grandmother's Flower Garden | DATE: c. 1940 | MAKER: **Ingeborg Vold Hara** | SIZE: 84" x 90" | OWNER: **Held in trust for Myrtle Hara and Ida Nysetvold by Orwin Nysetvold**

Ingeborg's beautiful depiction of a classic Grandmother's Flower Garden quilt.

Diamond Field ZigZag | DATE: c. 1940 | MAKER: **Ingeborg Vold Hara** | SIZE: 79" x 87" | OWNER: **Held in trust for Myrtle Hara and Ida Nysetvold by Orwin Nysetvold**

Ingeborg liked to experiment with different designs using the hexagon shape.

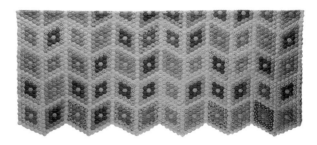

HONEYCOMB QUILT

Another Hexagon silk quilt that was documented in Minnesota (although it was made in Mendoza, Texas) is a Honeycomb pattern in the dark colors typical of the late nineteenth century. Family history attributes it to Ingeborg Charlotte Stromberg, since she was "the only one in the family impractical enough to make a quilt from silk."[2] The hexagons in this quilt measure one inch, and each bouquet measures thirteen inches. The back of the quilt is turkey-red cotton, and the quilting outlines the hexagons. Newspaper served as the paper for piecing and is still present inside the quilt.

Ingeborg's parents immigrated to the United States in 1870. They returned to Sweden for a visit in 1878, and Ingeborg was born while they were there. She lived all her life in and around Austin, Texas, with her mother and then with a sister and brother-in-law. Her profession as a milliner may have influenced her silk quilt, as the linings of hats were frequently silk and the scraps would be readily available to her. Carolyn Abbott, Ingeborg's great-niece, inherited the quilt twenty-nine years ago. When Carolyn was a child, she met Ingeborg, and she cherishes the handiwork of her great-aunt.

THE HEXAGON QUILTS OF INGEBORG WOLD HARA

Some quilters discovered that the Hexagon pattern was varied enough to allow them to experiment with

it time and again. One of those quilters in Minnesota was Ingeborg Wold Hara. Ingeborg was born in Norway in 1880 and came alone to North Dakota in 1902 to establish a homestead. In 1904, at the age of twenty-four, she married Christoffer Hara. They lived in several places in North Dakota before settling in Willmar, Minnesota, in 1920. The couple had four children.

Ingeborg began quilting after her marriage. She had become blind in her right eye at the age of four, so all of her fine quilting work was done with the sight of only one eye. The family knows of at least nine traditional quilts that Ingeborg made, plus many tied Crazy quilts. Ingeborg died in 1965 and her daughters, Myrtle Hara and Ida Nysetvold, have carefully preserved her quilts.

Ingeborg used the Hexagon pattern to create a classic Grandmother's Flower Garden, around 1940. A carefully planned color scheme radiates from a center yellow flower. The outer ring repeats the yellow flowers to complete the quilt.

In the first half of the twentieth century, magazines and newspapers were a way for Minnesota quilters to maintain a connection with current fashions and trends in the quilting world. Ingeborg used a pattern from a magazine to make her Diamond Field quilt, an unusual variation that creates an illusion of a folding screen.

Above: Hexagon Bouquet pattern from the Comfort Company in Augusta, Maine, c. 1940

Left: Clara used a commercial pattern from the Comfort Company in Maine and green fabric from the Montgomery Ward catalog to make her hexagon quilt.

Hexagon Bouquet | DATE: **1942** | SIZE: **83" x 91"** | MAKER: **Clara Louise Gregersen Jenkins** | OWNER: **Clara Louise Gregersen Jenkins**

HEXAGON BOUQUET QUILT

Clara Jenkins used a commercial pattern to create her Hexagon quilt, Hexagon Bouquet. She still has the pattern that she ordered in 1941, probably from a newspaper or magazine. The pattern came from the Comfort Company in Augusta, Maine, posted with a one-cent stamp.

Clara's Hexagon Bouquet quilt contains scraps from her handmade dresses and her mother's clothing, plus scraps that she requested from her friends. The green is a typical 1930s green that she remembers purchasing from Montgomery Ward by mail. The back is also green. Carefully handpieced and handquilted, this Hexagon quilt reflects the style of its time and the loving work of its creator.

Clara was born in Little Falls, Minnesota, in 1912. She was trained as a teacher and taught in one-room schoolhouses until after her marriage. Clara married Arthur Jenkins, and they had one son, Allen. When Arthur died in 1945, Clara returned to teaching. She taught for twenty-two years in northern Minnesota, returning each summer to the Fort Ripley area.

Clara began quilting in 1937 and is still quilting today. She has made more than one hundred quilts in her lifetime, giving them to her family or selling them to friends and neighbors. Clara is active in the Pinetree Patchworkers guild in Brainerd, Minnesota, and continues to find challenges in her quilting.

Tumbling Blocks

The sixty-degree diamond that is used to create the Tumbling Blocks quilt, also known as Baby Block, is similar in some ways to the Hexagon. This design is an arrangement of diamond-shaped pieces that are set to look like a three-dimensional cube or a block. The earliest example of this quilt, dated 1854, was documented by Barbara Brackman,[3] but the same pattern appears in the April 1850 issue of *Godey's*,[4] although it is not referred to by name. In the same article, the Hexagon block appeared. *Godey's* advised that the blocks should be made using the English paper piecing method, preferably with silk.

TUMBLING BLOCK QUILT

This Tumbling Block example was made around 1900, and the maker is unknown. One face of each block is a small sixty-degree Nine Patch block, which gives even more dimension to the quilt. Each four-inch-square block was handpieced and made from multi-colored scraps. The blue and red diamond shapes are English paper pieced.

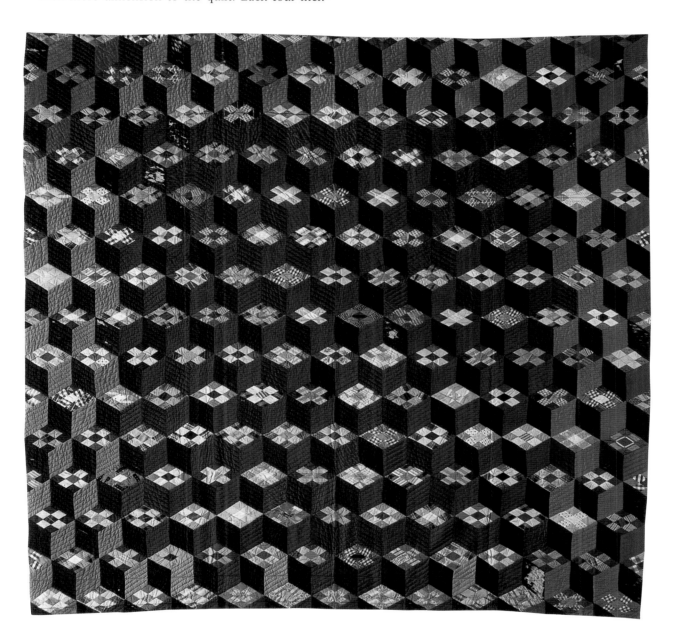

Tumbling Block variation | DATE: **c. 1900** | MAKER: **Unknown** | SIZE: **81" x 86"** | OWNER: **Hennepin History Museum**

An unknown quilter used a combination of traditional handpiecing and English paper piecing to create this stunning design.

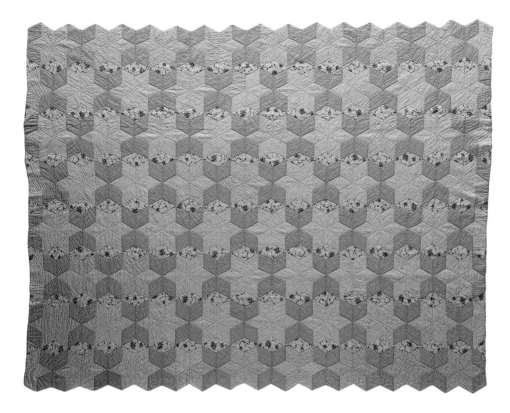

Star and Blocks | Date: c. 1945 | Maker: Hilda Erickson Lanning (1894–1985) | Size: 70" x 85" | Owner: Eleanor Throngard

Hilda's color placement in this Tumbling Block variation creates a star design.

Star and Blocks Quilt

Tumbling Blocks quilts made of cotton fabric were popular throughout the twentieth century. As in this green and yellow quilt, color placement can create a totally different look. This variation is called Star and Blocks. You have to look hard to see the tumbling blocks because of the strong star pattern. The quilt is machine pieced and handquilted.

Hilda Erickson Lanning made this quilt around 1940. She was born in 1884, in Erickson Township, Renville County, Minnesota, and it was there that she made the quilt. Hilda was the youngest of twelve children and grew up on a farm. She married Otto Lanning, a farmer, and they had one child, Eleanor. Her daughter estimates that Hilda made between twenty-five and thirty quilts.

Crazy Quilts

Crazy quilts were all the rage in the late 1800s, and they were the most abundant style of quilt found during Minnesota Quilt Project's Quilt Discovery Days.

The first descriptions of this new type of needlework, appearing in popular women's magazines, were rather vague, and the quilts didn't have a specific name.

The Crazy quilt craze peaked in the mid 1880s. The increase in the supply of silk from both American and foreign manufacturers may have helped boost the Crazy quilt's popularity. Fashionable magazines of the time included numerous ads for Crazy quilt silks. In 1887, *Godey's* wrote: "The time, patience, stitches and mistakes the crazy quilt represents are too awful for words."

Despite the harsh criticism, Crazy quilts remained popular with quiltmakers into the twentieth century. Later versions were often less ornate, with fewer decorative stitches and embellishments. The designs were modified to use fabrics that were durable and warm, and these utilitarian quilts were simply pieced, often with little or no decorative stitching.

The Crazy quilt inspired many poems, songs, and even a play, *Billy Rose's Crazy Quilt*, which opened on Broadway on May 19, 1931. The play was a musical revue, and one of the cast members was Fanny Brice.

CRAZY QUILT WITH STRING DESIGN

This quilt is a combination Crazy and String-pieced design. The blocks are arranged to form diamond patterns that are surrounded by crazy patches. The chevron borders on two sides contain the bold blocks while adding motion to the quilt's appearance. The fabrics are mostly silk, satin, and velvet.

The quiltmaker, Emily C. Johnson Swanson, was born in Sweden in 1856. She came to America when she was nineteen and worked as a hired girl and a cook before she married. She and her husband, Emil Swanson, had three children. He deserted the family when the children were still young and left Emily to raise them by herself. She returned to work as a cook and a maid to support her family.

The quilt is initialed (ES) but not dated. It is estimated to have been made around 1890. By planning or coincidence, the quilt contains many blue and yellow fabrics, which are the colors of the Swedish flag. It was passed down through the family and now belongs to Emily's granddaughter.

Crazy variation | DATE: c. 1885 | MAKER: Emily Johnson Swanson (1856–1934) | SIZE: 63" x 76" | OWNER: Evelyn Rydeen

Emily worked hard to support her family, but she managed to find time for creative endeavors, such as this beautiful Crazy quilt.

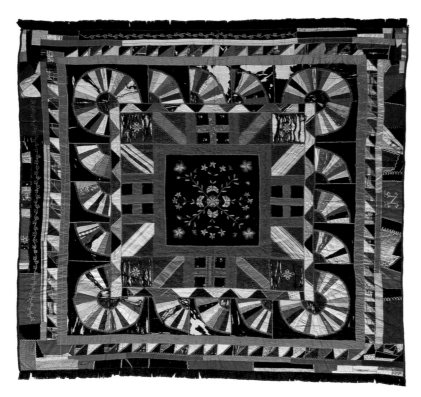

Above: Nellie, at about the time she made the two quilts.

Left: Nellie made two of these quilts; one of them was donated to a Red Cross auction during World War I.

Crazy variation | DATE: c. 1905 | MAKER: Nellie Onsgard Hallan (1887–1972) | SIZE: 70" x 74" | OWNER: Houston County Historical Society

SAWTOOTHED BORDER CRAZY QUILT

Although many Crazy quilts are random in design, the Crazy quilt made by Nellie Onsgard Hallan appears to have been carefully planned. It has a richly embroidered medallion center that is surrounded by sixteen pieced blocks and a triangle border. Carefully arranged Fan blocks wrap around the triangle border. The Fans are enclosed with a solid-colored narrow border, which is in turn surrounded by a sawtooth border. The final, outer border consists of randomly pieced scraps. Black ruffles on two opposite ends add a final flourish.

Nellie was born in 1887 in Spring Grove, Minnesota. Her parents settled in the area in 1864, and Nellie was a lifelong resident. In 1906, Nellie married banker Oscar Hallan, and they later had five daughters.

The amazing thing is that Nellie made two of these complicated Crazy quilts between 1902 and 1905. During World War I, Nellie donated one of the quilts to a Red Cross auction, as a fundraiser. The quilt went to the highest bidder for $25.

The quilt that Nellie kept was displayed in the spare room of her home, according to her daughters.

After her death in 1972, the family donated the quilt to the Houston County Historical Society in Caledonia, Minnesota.

CRAZY QUILT WITH LILAC MEDALLION

Crazy quilts often contained symbols and pictures that had a special meaning to the maker. This Crazy quilt provides a lot of information but, unfortunately, not the name of the maker. It is dated "1887" and "1889." This might mean that it was started in 1887 and finished in 1889, or it may be that the dates are significant for reasons known only to the quiltmaker. Many people and places are alluded to on the quilt. In addition to the two dates, the quilt includes the following embroidered and painted clues to its history:

St. Paul   New Durham, NJ

L.E.   AMG

Trenton, NJ.   LC

L. Beck   Rose

K.G.   F.W.N.G.

Rest $ M. Beck

The quilt has a black center medallion that is embellished with sprigs of lilac. The borders are embroidered with white roses, leaves, and ferns. The Crazy patches are also abundantly embellished with hand-painting, appliqué, and embroidery, including ribbon embroidery and ruching. The fabrics are primarily velvet and silk.

Crazy | DATE: c. 1889 | MAKER: Unknown | SIZE: 60" x 64" | OWNER: Sibley House Historic Site

This lavish Crazy quilt, made by an unknown quiltmaker, contains many intriguing clues to its origins.

Left: Embroidered and painted motifs lavishly decorate this quilt.

Pineapple Log Cabin | DATE: **c. 1880** | MAKER: **Henrietta Fredrick Pritzel (1836–1926)** | SIZE: **72"x 74"** | OWNER: **Eileen Pritzel Tank**

Henrietta made this Pineapple Log Cabin quilt as a wedding present for her grandson.

Log Cabin Quilts

During Minnesota's Quilt Discovery Days, Log Cabin quilts ranked fourth in popularity of all the quilts brought in for documentation. The first Log Cabin quilts appeared in the United States in the early 1800s, but the style didn't peak in popularity until the time of the Civil War. Log Cabin quilts have remained popular ever since. One reason for the Log Cabin's popularity may be that it has so many variations. Some of the more well-known settings include Barn Raising, Courthouse Steps, Streak of Lightning, Sunshine and Shadow, and Straight Furrow.

The center of the Log Cabin block is traditionally red, signifying the cabin chimney, but the center piece varies depending upon available fabric and the quiltmaker's preference. The strips, or logs, are easily adaptable to wool, cotton, or silk, and the block is usually pieced onto a square of inexpensive or recycled foundation fabric, such as muslin.

Log cabin quilts can be separated into two broad groups, according to the fabric used and the purpose of the quilt. The first group includes the more practical quilts made of cotton or wool. These quilts were meant to be utilitarian, but many were also enjoyed for their beauty. They varied in size from crib quilts, to "hired man" bed size, to coverings for large, family-sized beds in the pioneer log cabins.

The second group of Log Cabin quilts was popular during the late nineteenth to early twentieth century, when Crazy quilts were all the rage. These Log Cabin quilts were made with silk, satin, and velvet fabrics and were often used to accessorize a room, rather than be functional.

PINEAPPLE LOG CABIN QUILTS

Henrietta Fredrick Pritzel, born in 1836 in New York State, made this primarily red and blue Log Cabin Pineapple quilt in the 1880s. She gave the quilt as a wedding present to her grandson, Benjamin Pritzel, and his bride, Gertrude Haase. Eileen Pritzel Tank, Henrietta's great-granddaughter, now owns the quilt.

Another example of a Log Cabin Pineapple quilt is this two-color quilt. Quiltmaker Helga Slotten Cole purchased new fabric for it and completed the machine piecing and handquilting in 1922. Helga was born in

Norway in 1881 and was a pastry cook and a seamstress there, making clothes for the upper class. (According to a family story, she even sewed for a princess.)

In 1902, she came to America to visit her cousin. In those days, transoceanic visits usually lasted several months. During the visit, Helga found work as a seamstress and met her cousin's brother-in-law, Christian Cole. They fell in love and got married. Christian was a farmer, and the couple homesteaded in Yellow Medicine County, Minnesota.

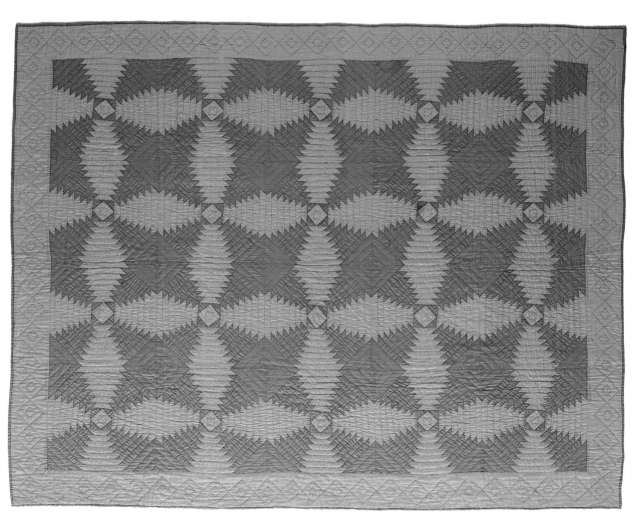

Pineapple Log Cabin | DATE: 1922 | MAKER: Helga Slotten Cole (1881–1947) | SIZE: 68" x 82" | OWNER: Harriet Velde

Helga purchased all new fabric in 1922 for her Pineapple Log Cabin quilt.

Barn Raising Log Cabin | DATE: **c. 1900** | MAKER: **Attributed to Mrs. William Windhorst** | SIZE: **72" x 92"** | OWNER: **Renville County History Museum**

Red and blue wool were used to make this Barn Raising Log Cabin quilt—definitely a winter quilt!

BARN RAISING LOG CABIN

This bold red and blue Log Cabin has forty-eight blocks set in the Barn Raising design. The quilt, believed to have been made by Mrs. William Windhorst around 1900, is wool. The quiltmaker's husband owned the first lumber mill in Renville County, Minnesota, and the family was one of the first to settle there. Barbara Witt, the granddaughter of the quiltmaker, donated the quilt to the Renville County History Museum.

Log Cabin, Cross Within a Cross variation | DATE: c. 1890 | MAKER: Unknown | SIZE: 53" x 54" | OWNER: Winona County Historical Society

An unknown quiltmaker used cotton, silk, wool, and velvet to create this Cross Within a Cross setting.

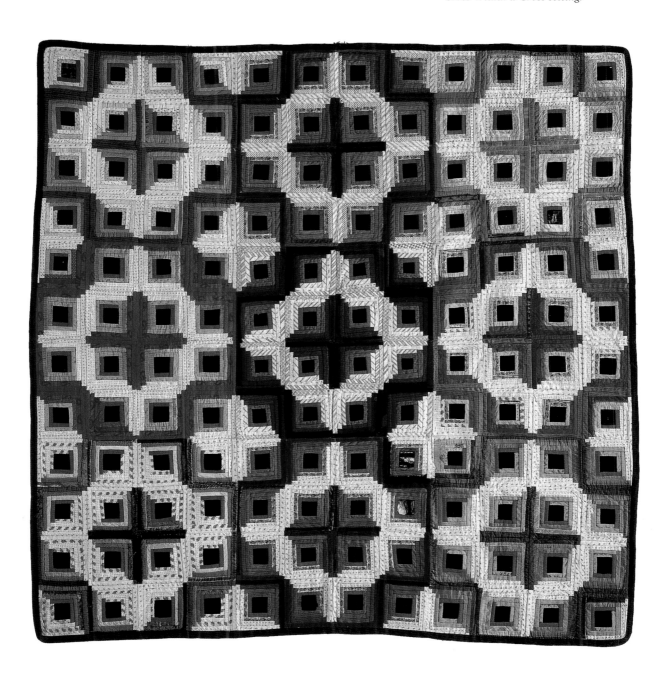

CROSS WITHIN A CROSS LOG CABIN

There is little information about this quilt, which is part of the Winona County Historical Society collection. The Log Cabin setting, Cross Within a Cross, is not a common Log Cabin design, requiring creativity and planning to have the design come together correctly. The quilt top, made between 1875 and 1900, includes cotton, silk, wool, and velvet. The 144 blocks are four-inches square.

Fan Quilts

Fan quilts were often made out of silk during the same time period that elaborate Crazy quilts and silk Log Cabin quilts were popular, between 1880 and 1900. The style was also popular from 1920 until 1940, when quilters often used feed-sack material to create the brightly colored fan. The quarter circle in each fan block was typically the same fabric throughout the quilt.

Grandmother's Fan Quilt
There are many different settings for Fan quilts. This quilt, made by Helen Kollin Homme, around 1920, represents one of the most popular settings, Grandmother's Fan. The quilt features large feathers, handquilted with blue thread in each block.

Helen was born in 1882 in rural Belleview, Minnesota. Before she married Torjus Homme, she was a schoolteacher. The couple had one child, Grant. Helen was an active member of the Rock Valle Lutheran Church Ladies Aid, and she made many quilts to donate to the church's Mission Day Sale. This event started in 1877 and continues to this day. Maysel Homme, Helen's daughter-in-law, now owns the quilt.

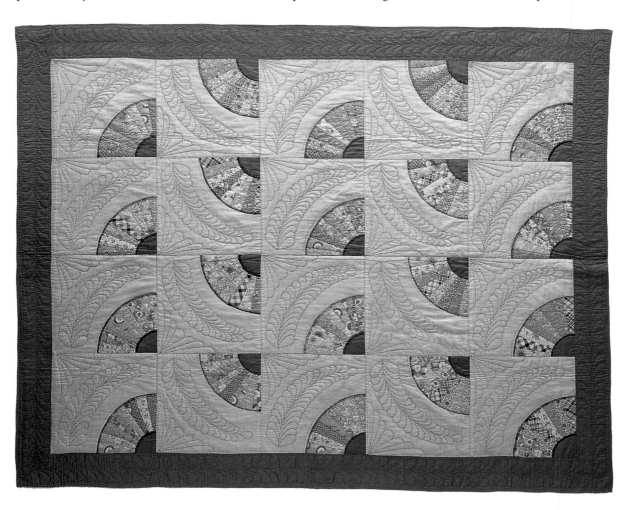

Grandmother's Fan | Date: c. 1920 | Maker: Helen Kollin Homme
Size: 70" x 90" | Owner: Maysel Homme

Helen used blue thread to handquilt feathers in the large, open areas surrounding the fans.

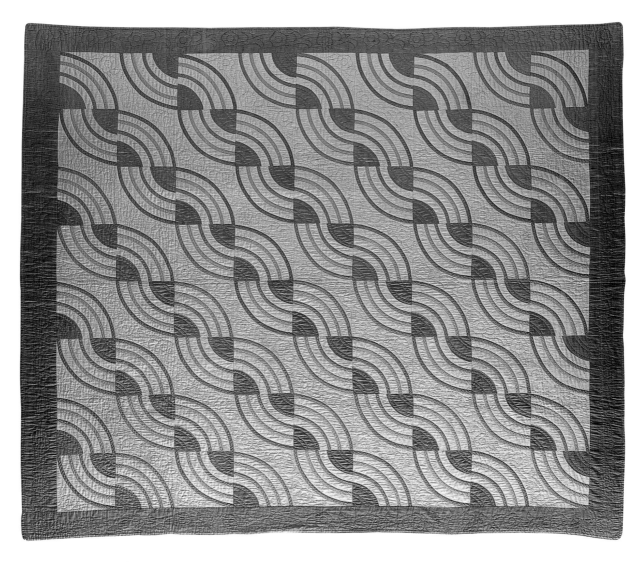

Fan, Rainbow variation | DATE: c. 1930 | MAKER: Louisa Crozier Hill (1874–1954) | SIZE: 72" x 81" | OWNER: John and Catherine Hill

Lottie taught herself how to quilt in her late forties and made many quilts in her lifetime, including this Fan quilt.

RAINBOW FAN QUILT

Another Fan quilt, made around 1930 by Louisa Crozier Hill, has a very different look. The quilt, made with solid-colored cotton, is handpieced, appliquéd with bias strips, and handquilted.

Louisa (Lottie) was born in 1874 in White Bear Lake, Minnesota. She went to school through the eighth grade before attending the Conservatory of Music in Toronto, Ontario. She completed her studies and taught piano until she married John James Hill.

According to their son, John, Lottie taught herself to quilt when she was almost fifty. She won many prizes for her quilts and used the prize money to buy more fabric. She would say, "I'd rather have a needle in my hand than a fork—and I'm mighty good with a fork." She liked quilting with friends, and they helped her quilt the tops that she pieced for her sons' dowries. John and his wife, Catherine, have many of the quilts that Lottie made.

Above: Did the symbol stitched in red on this quilt have a special meaning, or was Mary just being creative?

Double Wedding Ring | DATE: c. 1920 | MAKER: Mary Dube O'Marro (1890–1965) | SIZE: 67" x 94" | OWNER: Rose Mary Wright

Mary made this quilt soon after escaping from the Cloquet area Great Fire of 1918.

Double Wedding Ring Quilts

As with many quilt patterns, there is some debate about the origin of the Double Wedding Ring pattern and when it first appeared. *Capper's Weekly* first published the Double Wedding Ring pattern in 1928, and it was very popular for the decade or two that followed the publication. However, there are earlier versions of the pattern, and it was undoubtedly one that quiltmakers shared among themselves long before it was published in *Capper's*.

Interlocking rings have been a popular motif for centuries, although exchanging wedding rings is a fairly recent custom. Therefore, earlier quilts of this design had names that did not have anything to do with wedding rings. Pre-twentieth-century versions of the pattern had a variety of names, including Rainbow, Around the World, Endless Chain, King Tut, and Friendship Knot.

APPLIQUÉD DOUBLE WEDDING RING QUILT
In some early Double Wedding Ring quilts, quiltmakers appliquéd the rings onto solid fabric rather than piecing the rings and background together. That is how this quilt was constructed. The appliquéd rings are made of multicolored scraps in predominantly red and blue. The quiltmaker added the red embroidery, which is decorative and also holds the layers together. There is no batting. When asked about the unusual embroidery design, the quiltmaker's granddaughter said that her grandmother was "very creative and always had lots of ideas."

The quiltmaker was Mary Dube O'Marro. She was born in 1890 in the lumber mill town of Cloquet, Minnesota, where her parents settled in the late nineteenth century. Her parents came from Canada and were of Scotch and French ancestry. According to family members, Mary was the first female child born in the town of Cloquet, which was home to very few women at that time.

Mary survived the Great Fire of 1918 that totally destroyed the town of Cloquet and other towns and farms in that area. More than four hundred people died, but the people of Cloquet survived due the fast action of the town's stationmaster. When he knew that the fire was heading towards the town and was wiping out everything in its path, he telegraphed the railroad yard in Duluth, Minnesota (twenty miles away and not in the fire's path). He asked them to send all of the empty boxcars that they had. The boxcars were quickly transported to Cloquet where the townspeople were waiting to board them. There was enough room for all

of the town's residents, and nobody from Cloquet perished in the fire.

Before the fire, Mary had worked at the Wright Hotel, but after the town was rebuilt, she owned and managed her own establishment, the Dube Hotel, in downtown Cloquet.

GUNTER FAMILY DOUBLE WEDDING RING QUILT
Another early-twentieth-century Double Wedding Ring was made around 1910 by Clara Langon Gunter. Born in 1876 in Rock Valley, Iowa, she moved to Clara City, Minnesota, after her marriage to Tom Gunter. They had six children and farmed in the Clara City area. Clara's quilt has a graphic simplicity that conveys a certain charm. She presented it to her son, John M. Gunter, and his new wife, Marcella Priebe Gunter, when they married in 1941. Marcella said that at that time it was in need of some repair, which she did herself. The quilt has been used and loved, and it is now a treasured keepsake.

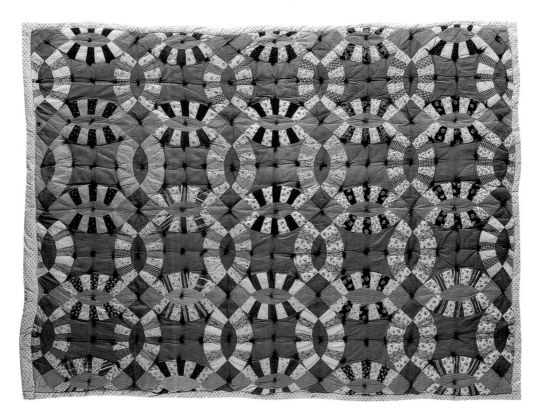

Double Wedding Ring | DATE: c. 1910 | MAKER: Clara Langan Gunter (1876–1960) | SIZE: 64" x 81" | OWNER: Marcella Gunter

As a young farm wife with six children, Clara probably made this quilt to be utilitarian, but she also managed to make it colorful and charming.

Irish Chain Quilts

The Irish Chain pattern has been popular throughout American quilt history. It can be created as a scrap quilt with single, double, or triple chains, or as a precisely designed, color-coordinated quilt. Elaborate or simple quilting, trapunto, and appliqué designs sometimes ornament the alternate squares. In Minnesota, more than eighty-six Irish Chain quilts have been documented.

Research by quilt historians indicates that the earliest Irish Chain quilt was made in America in the early 1800s and that the pattern originated here. However, a quilt brought to West Virginia from Ireland in 1807 was very similar to the single Irish Chain quilt and may have been the basis for the design.

DOUBLE IRISH CHAIN QUILTS

Ruth Green of Murray County, Minnesota, related a tradition of Irish Chains within her family. She brought two Irish Chains to be documented: one a green and peach double Irish Chain made by her grandmother, Gertrude Dodd Lovell, and the other a doll-size Irish Chain made by Nancy DeBois Stevens, Gertrude's maternal grandmother.

Nancy Dubois Stevens, maker of the doll quilt

Double Irish Chain doll quilt | DATE: 1858 | MAKER: Nancy Dubois Stevens (?–1861) | SIZE: 19" x 19" | OWNER: Ruth Green

Double Irish Chain quilt | DATE: Began in 1931, quilted in 1941 | MAKER: Pieced by Gertrude Dodd Lovell, quilted by two ladies with the surname of Oliver | SIZE: 74" x 84" | OWNER: Ruth Green

The doll quilt made by Nancy Stevens rests on top of the full size quilt made by her granddaughter, Gertrude Lovell.

Grant and Gertrude Dodd; Gertrude received the doll quilt

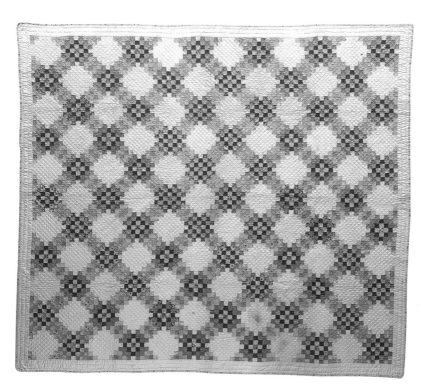

The yellow fabric used in this quilt came from a dress that Zelda wore to the Chicago World's Fair in 1933.

In 1857, Gertrude's father, Tomas Dodd, a schoolteacher who lived in New York City, felt the call to go west. His wife Elizabeth's family had a tradition that each girl was given an Irish Chain quilt. Since there was not enough time for a full quilt to be made for Gertrude before the trip west, her grandmother, Nancy, made her a doll quilt, which was to serve as a pattern for a full-size quilt. Gertrude had a little trunk, and she kept her doll and her quilt in it as her family traveled west in a covered wagon. These items are still in the family's possession. The Dodds spent time in Wisconsin and Illinois before 1863 when they settled in Martin County, Minnesota, where Thomas became a circuit rider for the Presbyterian Church.

In this photograph, the little quilt made by Nancy in 1857 rests on the larger quilt made by Gertrude in 1931. Gertrude made the quilt for her granddaughter, Ruth, and it is the only quilt that she ever made. Ruth has continued the tradition by giving Irish Chain quilts to both of her granddaughters. Gertrude, Ruth's mother, Bessie, and Ruth all played with the little Irish Chain quilt. Ruth says, "My grandmother Gertrude died at the age of 84, when I was eight years old. I remember my brother and I perching on the arms of her chair to hear wonderful stories of early days in Minnesota. She told of riding horseback through the tall prairie grass, of the untimely deaths of her two brothers, leaving her the only child, and of the little quilt."[5]

POSTAGE STAMP TRIPLE IRISH CHAIN QUILT
Zelda Detert, born in 1912 in Northrup, Minnesota, made her postage stamp Triple Irish Chain in the mid 1930s. This is a multiple scrap quilt, related to the earliest Irish Chain quilts. The yellow fabric in this quilt is from a dress that Zelda wore to the Chicago World's Fair in 1933. The quilt contains almost five thousand pieces, each measuring one inch. Zelda is very proud of this fine example of her machine piecing. (The alternate corners were applied by hand.)

According to Zelda, "We girls in our neighborhood all made quilts in those years. It was the rage. We didn't have much to do. Well, it was the depression. So we would get together to make quilts and quilt them. My mother and sister and I quilted our special quilts, though. I was kind of fussy about the quilting in those."[6]

The mid 1930s was the peak of Zelda's quilting career. In 1937, she and her husband, Dietreck, moved to a new farm. Sadly, the amount of work that needed to be done to run the farm did not allow any time for quilting.

Double Irish Chain | DATE: **1940s** | MAKER: **Katherina Reding Moser (1877–1968)** | SIZE: **71" x 90"** | OWNER: **Jeannette Root**

Kate transformed bleached and handdyed plain feed sacks into this classic two-color Irish Chain quilt.

TWO COLOR IRISH CHAIN QUILT

Katherina Reding Moser made this quilt, as the Irish Chain pattern continued to be popular into the 1940s. Katherina (Kate) was born in Switzerland in 1877 and came to the United States in 1892 at fifteen years of age. In 1894, she married Frank Moser; they had ten children. She and Frank lived on a series of farms in the area around the Twin Cities. When Frank died, she continued to farm with the help of her children. At the age of thirty, she became deaf; she was able to lip read and communicated with pen and paper.

One day in 1936 her house caught fire. Kate threw clothes and quilts out the windows. According to the family story, she thought that if the family had enough quilts, they could sleep in the barn until the house was rebuilt.

Kate always insisted that she go with her husband or sons to the feed store so that she could pick out her own feed sacks for quilts. To find time to quilt with the heavy work of farming, she would rise at 4 A.M. and quilt for an hour before milking the cows. In the winter, she hosted quilting bees.

Kate made many quilts in her lifetime, but they were well used and not many are left today. She passed on her love of quilting to her granddaughters, helping them at their quilt frames even when she was in her eighties. She died in 1968 at the age of ninety-one. Reminiscing about her grandmother, Jeannette Root says, "Her life is a reflection of the pioneer spirit of the women of that time."[7]

Kate's two-color Irish Chain consists of bleached white and home-dyed blue feed sacks. It is hand and machine pieced. A lovely cone border with a scalloped edge adds a lyric frame to the diagonal strength of the chain. Kate wanted to be sure that her quilting patterns were easy to see, so she quilted with blue perle cotton.

Star Quilts

Star quilt patterns have been documented in the United States as early as the late eighteenth century.[8] The first known name for a quilt with one large pieced star in the center is believed to be Mathematical Star, and the name probably originated in England. Later names for this quilt include Star of Bethlehem, Blazing Star, and Lone Star. The star comprised many small diamonds, radiating from the center, carefully arranged and pieced. The early Star quilts (those made around 1800) were often medallion-style quilts surrounded by pieced blocks, borders, or appliqué designs, such as Broderie Perse. Later in the nineteenth century, the star grew to cover the entire quilt top, with piecing or appliqué to fill the corners and the spaces between the star points.

LONE STAR AND LEMOYNE STAR QUILT

This Lone Star, or Star of Bethlehem, was made by Sarah Nelson Moline. Whole and half Lemoyne stars on a purple background surround the center star. The back of the quilt is a small, lavender and white floral print.

Sarah was born in 1871 in East Union, Minnesota. Before her marriage, she was a clerk in her brother's general store in Elk River, Minnesota. (The building is still standing and now houses a restaurant.) She married John Moline later in life and never had any children. The many quilts that Sarah made, all handpieced and handquilted, were passed on to her nieces.

Lone Star and Lemoyne Stars | DATE: c. 1920 | MAKER: Sarah Nelson Moline (1871–1939) | SIZE: 66" x 72" | OWNER: Catherine Wornson

Sarah probably purchased new purple fabric for this quilt, possibly from her brother's general store.

Blazing Star | DATE: c. 1940 | Quilter: Pauline Ringwelski Copa (1881– 1971) | SIZE: 73" x 91" | OWNER: Jane Tillman Shaw

In color and design, this is the epitome of a Blazing Star quilt.

BLAZING STAR QUILT

Another variation of the Lone Star is this Blazing Star in vibrant yellow, with pink, blue, and green. Pauline Ringwelski Copa, who was born in Poland in 1881, made the quilt. She immigrated to the United States as a young child with her family. The family settled in Morrison County, Minnesota, which had a large population of Polish immigrants. Pauline and her husband, Vincent Copa, had ten children. Pauline was living in Little Falls, Minnesota, when she made this quilt, which she machine pieced and handquilted.

SIX-POINTED MEDALLION STAR QUILT

Every state documentation project has its share of mystery quilts. These quilts have usually been purchased at auctions, flea markets, and garage sales, with no information about their makers. One such quilt is this unusual six-pointed, large medallion star, pieced in the style of a Lone Star. It is both machine and hand-pieced, and the quilting was done by machine. The colors that surround the star and its white, hexagon background are muted and somewhat somber. The quilt's owner lives in central Minnesota, but there is no clue as to where the quilt came from originally. The solid-colored fabrics make this quilt difficult to date, but it is estimated to have been made between 1920 and 1930.

Six-Pointed Medallion Star | **DATE:** 1920s | **MAKER:** Unknown | **SIZE:** 68" x 86" | **OWNER:** Beverly Keltgen

This understated but sophisticated quilt was made by an unknown quilter, using large pieces of various solid-colored fabric.

Feathered Star | Date: **c. 1900** | Maker: **Mrs. Goodman** | Size: **72" x 84"** | Owner: **Pipestone County Historical Society**

This challenging Feathered Star quilt is surrounded by a border of Lily blocks.

Feathered Star Quilt

The Feathered Star pattern began to appear in quilts in the early nineteenth century. The basic Feathered Star block contains small triangles that "feather" the points of the stars, and the pattern is usually only attempted and completed by an experienced quilter.

The current owner bought this Feathered Star quilt from Opal Denhart Brenan. The quiltmaker was Opal's grandmother, known to the owner only as Mrs. Good-

man, and the quilt was passed to Opal by her mother, known only as Mrs. John Denhart. It consists of twenty Feathered Star blocks surrounded on three sides by a wide border of Lily blocks. A different block defines each of the two corners where the borders meet, a Lemoyne Star and a Carolina Lily. It's possible that Mrs. Goodman ran out of fabrics and substituted the Lemoyne Star block from her sample blocks.

Whole Cloth Quilts

There were sixty-four whole cloth quilts discovered in Minnesota, and several were unusual. Whole cloth quilts, the oldest style of quilts, are defined as two layers of cloth joined together by decorative stitching with some kind of wadding (batting) in between. The earliest known European whole cloth quilt exists in Sicily, and it is believed to have been made during the fourteenth century. By the eighteenth century, whole cloth quilts were produced both professionally and at home in most of Europe and in the United States. The quilts were a symbol of status and good taste.

At the beginning of the nineteenth century, white work whole cloth quilts became increasingly popular. These were often associated with the term "bride's quilt" and were considered to be the greatest challenge to a quilter's skill. Although not as numerous as other styles of quilts, wonderful examples exist in excellent condition. After spending several years of her

Whole cloth quilt, made in Norway | **DATE: c. 1775** | **MAKERS: Anna Margarethe Munthe (1758–1839); Anna Catharine Munthe, Mette Andrea Christine Munthe (1762–?)** | **SIZE: 82" x 87"** | **OWNER: Minnesota Historical Society**

A sumptuous silk quilt made in Norway is an elegant example of a whole cloth quilt. (Courtesy of the Minnesota Historical Society)

life quilting an exquisite pattern, a quiltmaker would treat her masterpiece with the utmost care, and the family who inherited it often continued to treasure and care for it.

NORWEGIAN WHOLE CLOTH QUILT

An early example of a whole cloth quilt came to Minnesota from Norway. Family history dates this quilt to 1775 and suggests it was made by three sisters or sisters-in-law, Mette Andrea Christine Munthe, Anna Catharine Munthe, and Anna Margarethe Munthe. Anna Margarethe became the grandmother of Ole Bull (1810–1880), the famous Norwegian violinist.

Mette became the owner of the quilt. She married Christopher Juel in about 1790, and the eldest daughter in each generation after her inherited the quilt. Her great-grandson, Tollief George Thomsen, received the quilt because there were no girls born to his parents. He brought it with him when he pioneered in Aitkin County, Minnesota, in 1882. Marie Thomsen received the quilt from her father, Tollief, and donated it to the Minnesota Historical Society in 1964.

The quilt has an apple-green silk top and a block-printed backing. The printed design on the back consists of red flowers and black leaf tracery. It is quilted with silk thread at approximately ten top stitches per inch, through a wool batt of medium thickness. The silk panels are thirteen inches wide, and thirteen yards of silk were required to make this quilt. A medallion circle rose is framed by half and quarter circles to create a rectangular center. Each of the three succeeding borders is quilted in a unique pattern, which are variations on curvilinear designs. Four corner blocks seem to be quadrant hearts in echo quilting. An upholstery-style woven tape is secured to the top of the quilt as decoration on three sides; it appears that the tape was originally on all four sides.

The total effect is of a formal, intricate, and sophisticated design. The richness of the fabric, the use of silk thread, and the complexity of the pattern indicates that the Munthe family was well-to-do and in tune with fashions of the period.

WHITE WORK WHOLE CLOTH QUILT

A unique white work quilt, decorated with embroidery, was believed to have been made by Isabella (Belle) Graham Hunter Gillespie, born in Jackson, Minnesota, in 1874. Her mother's family (Hunter) came to America from Scotland in the 1840s, and her father's family came west from New York after the Civil War. Both families settled first in Iowa and then in southern Minnesota. Belle's father purchased a hardware store in Jackson, which later became the Gillespie Our Own Hardware store. Belle had three children, Helen, Hunter, and Margaret. Margaret lived with her mother until Belle's death and remained in the family home until her own death.

One intriguing thing about this quilt is that it contains Mountmellic work, a white-on-white embroidery technique. Between 1900 and 1920, many needlework magazines carried patterns for Mountmellic work. According to Patsy and Myron Orlofsky in *Quilts in America*, "Other white-on-white embroidery techniques that have been used for counterpanes include Mountmellic work, which originated in Ireland in the 1830s and is considered a style as well as a technique."[9] It was an unusual technique to be used in a small town in Minnesota in the early 1900s. It is possible that Belle could have learned the technique from her Scottish mother.

Probably the most interesting thing about this quilt's story is that when the family estate was settled after both Margaret and Helen had died, a second, almost identical quilt was found. This raises the question: Was a quilt made for each daughter? One of the quilts was donated to the Minnesota Historical Society, while the other is treasured and cared for by Ted Kolderie and Kay White, Helen's children.

White work whole cloth quilt | Date: **c. 1915** | Maker: **Attributed to Belle Hunter Gillespie (1874–1954)** | Size: **81" x 86"** | Owners: **Ted Kolderie and Kay White, children of Helen Gillespie Kolderie**

This beautiful quilt has a twin that was hidden away for many years.

Chapter Six

Connections to Quilting Fads and Fancies of the Twentieth Century

BY PATRICIA COX

Minnesota quilters come from many ethnic backgrounds. Making one quilt or many, they were hardworking, often raising large families and working alongside their husbands to support the family. There were networks or groups of quilters, especially in small towns, who kept quilting alive during the years when it was not widely popular. Despite all the hardships, struggles, and successes, Minnesota quilters managed to keep up with the trends and fads, making a worthy contribution to the world of quilting. At times these fads may not have been considered important, but they are part of our quilting history and deserve as much attention as any other facet of quilting.

Some of the most popular quilting trends include Sunbonnet Sue quilts, redwork, cross-stitch kits, appliqué kit quilts, Dresden Plate quilts, and other common designs used during the middle of the twentieth century. During the Great Depression, scrap quilts became popular, as quilters recycled leftover fabric and old clothing to make quilts to keep the family warm.

Sunbonnet Sue Quilts

Sunbonnet Sue, a pattern much loved and sometimes maligned, is Minnesota's one claim to an original design. Many artists contributed to the character that would eventually be the focus of the Sunbonnet Sue pattern, but Betha Corbett is considered the originator of the design in Minnesota.

Bertha Corbett was born in 1872 in Denver, Colorado. She studied art in Minneapolis, Philadelphia, and Chicago. While she was working in Minneapolis as a *Minneapolis Journal* illustrator, a group of congenial artist friends challenged her to create an expressive figure without showing its face. Bertha accepted the challenge and created the first Sunbonnet Baby.

The babies, characterized by large bonnets that covered their face and hair, were enthusiastically received and became a major focus in Corbett's life. In 1900, she self-published *The Sun-Bonnet Babies*, a book that caught the attention of Eulalie Osgood Groves, a writer of children's school primers. Corbett became the illustrator of these primers. Her designs were also found on postcards, china, stationary, the Dutch Cleanser can, and other items. Her logo became a Sunbonnet Baby carrying a huge four-leaf clover. She also produced the book, *Over-all Boys*, but it was never as popular as *The Sun-Bonnet Babies*. She married George H. Melcher, and in 1910 they moved to California, where she continued to paint. She was an accomplished artist in both watercolor and oils, but she devoted most of her time to drawing her Sunbonnet Babies. The couple farmed in the Santa Monica area, and Bertha lived there until her death in 1950.

Artist Kate Greenaway (1846–1901) depicted young children, especially young girls in bonnets. She was a British book editor, but she also illustrated greeting cards and almanacs; many of her designs also appeared on Victorian crazy quilts. The book *Infant Amusements, or How to Make a Nursery Happy*, by William H. G. Kingston and illustrated by Greenaway, was published in 1867. Greenaway illustrated books until 1900, creating at least fifty-five illustrated books and countless magazine drawings. Her work was probably the inspiration for those who later drew Sunbonnet Babies, but Corbett's girls bear little resemblance to Kate's.

Another player in the Sunbonnet story was illustrator Bernhardt Wall, one of Bertha Corbett's contemporaries. There are distinct differences between Corbett's style and that of Wall. Each illustrator drew different bonnets, and Wall's girls did not wear aprons.

Quiltmaker Ruth Kapp

Sunbonnet Sue | DATE: c. 1920 | MAKER: Ruth Kapp | SIZE: 67" x 82" | OWNER: Mary Dullinger, niece

The treasured Sunbonnet Sue

According to Dolores Hinson's article "The Sunbonnet Family of Quilt Patterns," there were Sunbonnet designs for embroidery in the *Ladies Art Catalog* that replicate Wall's drawings, but there is no definite proof that Corbett's drawings were converted to patterns for sale.

Artists such as Grace Dayton, creator of the Cambell Soup Kids, didn't draw Sunbonnet Sues herself, but her commercial illustrations would later influence Sue's design. The children Dayton drew were plumper than the original Sunbonnet Sue, and after the Cambell Soup Kids became popular, a plumper version of Sunbonnet Sue began to appear. The Sunbonnet Sue of today is chubby with a simple bonnet and shoes. Sometimes she has an arm and sometimes not. Often the appliqué is edged with a black buttonhole stitch. Modern Sues are often stationary and do not have the charm of movement and the industriousness of Corbett's girls.

In 1981, Jean Cuddy, a dedicated quilter and organizer, held her fourth quilt show in Mankato, Minnesota. This one was dedicated to Sunbonnet Sue, because she was so important to Minnesota quilting history. Along with the many Sunbonnet Sues displayed, there was a special heritage quilt that consisted of blocks featuring Sunbonnet children made by quilters from all over the United States, including one by Jean Cuddy. Joyce Aufderheide, a nationally known quilter and quilt collector of New Ulm, Minnesota, and Betty Hagerman of Baldwin City, Kansas, who wrote the book *A Meeting of the Sunbonnet Children*, were both present at the show. Hagerman brought two Sunbonnet Sue quilts with her to display, and Cuddy's quilt "Country Cousins Gather in Town Square" was also part of the exhibit.

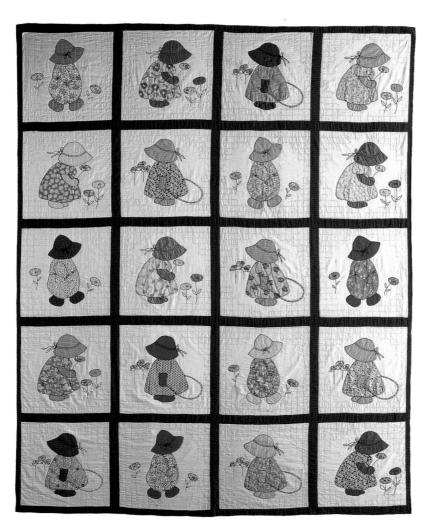

Sunbonnet Sue and Overall Bill
DATE: c. 1950 | MAKER: Minnie Scheffert, quilted by Minnie Scheffert, Esther Koepp, Emma and Lena Sieveke | SIZE: 75" x 95" | OWNER: Debra Adams, granddaughter

Both Sunbonnet Sue and Overall Bill are included in this quilt.

Below: *Bertha Corbett's Sunbonnet Children Days of the Week.*

SUNBONNET SUE

Ruth Kapp made several quilts that her family found in her cedar chest after she died. Sunbonnet Sue is one of several quilts, both finished and unfinished, found in the chest. Her brown sewing box contained cutout pieces for future work, but they will remain there in memory of her. The family felt the love and history that Ruth had stitched into each of the quilts as they lifted them up and examined them. The colors she used in her quilts reflect her love of gardening.

SUNBONNET SUE AND OVERALL BILL QUILT

Minnie Scheffert was a prolific quilter who made more than one hundred quilts in her lifetime. She learned the techniques from her mother and often quilted with her sisters, Esther Koepp and Lena and Emma Sieveke.

This quilt includes both Sunbonnet Sues and Overall Bills. In some of the blocks, the girls are jumping rope. All of the blocks are decorated with flowers.

Redwork

Redwork, straight line embroidery using red floss to create an outline stitch, was easier than some of the other embroidery techniques, making it very popular in the nineteenth and early twentieth centuries. The technique has experienced a revival in the late twentieth and early twenty-first centuries. Although the style has some English influences—namely the Kensington Royal School of Art Needlework, Briggs & Company, and Kate Greenaway designs—the craze was primarily American. During the late Victorian era, it became fashionable to decorate everything in sight, and the redwork trend inspired women to embroider all that could be embroidered. In addition to quilts, embroidery found its way on to many practical linens throughout the home, such as "splashers," cloths placed behind sinks and washbasins. "Good Morning" and "Good Night" appeared on numerous pillow shams and chair-back covers. Dish towels were decorated with days of the week, dishes, and cutlery patterns.

In 1874, Briggs & Company in Great Britain developed an iron-on transfer method that made it easier to place a design on fabric. Before iron-on transfers were available, quiltmakers tried various other methods. Stencils and perforated patterns, some made by hand using a pin to prick the holes, were popular. Quiltmakers then used chalk to "pounce" or dust over the perforations, penetrating the holes and marking the fabric. They would stabilize the lines by placing a piece of cloth over the chalked outlines and pressing them with a hot iron. This step had to be done carefully so as not to disturb the chalk.

Kate Greenaway Redwork Quilt

This redwork quilt by an unknown maker features embroidered Kate Greenaway designs. The provenance given the current owner when she purchased the quilt indicated that the quilt was completed over a ten-year period.

Redwork became popular with the introduction of embroidery floss colored with Turkey Red, which did not run. Developed in 1829, Turkey Red was far superior to sythetic dyes and was widely available by the end of the century. A similar, non-running blue dye was also introduced, although bluework showed up mostly after 1910. Red and blue were the most popular colors for embroidery work at the time, although examples of green, yellow, brown, and black work are known to have existed. Red, however, was favored because it was a bright and cheerful color.

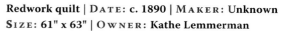

Redwork quilt | Date: c. 1890 | Maker: Unknown
Size: 61" x 63" | Owner: Kathe Lemmerman

Kathe Lemmerman is the proud owner of this redwork quilt, which features Kate Greenaway designs.

Because men were stronger, it was said that an angel gave women the gift of tears and a love of needlework as compensation.

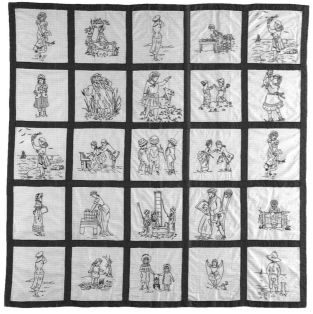

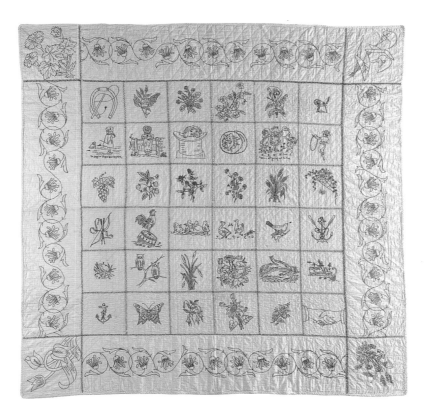

**Botanicals | Date: c. 1900
Maker: Ada Smith | Size: 68" x
69" | Owner: Judy Swift, a distant
cousin of the maker**

*This redwork quilt from Pennsylvania
features botanical patterns.*

Pennsylvania Redwork Quilt

Ada Smith made the top of this redwork quilt in Pennsylvania between 1900 and 1910. She gave it to a cousin, Marian Bender, who in turn passed it on to her daughter, Judy Swift. The quilt contains a mixture of patterns, many of which are botanicals, from various sources. The border is of special interest because it is a circular design encompassing a flower within each circle.

Before 1900, embroidery designs were seldom marketed for quilt blocks. Therefore, if the motif sizes are uniform, the quilt is generally dated after 1910, when embroidery designs began being applied to quilts. The variety and combination of design choices is what makes each of these redwork coverlets unique. Many were not quilted or even lined with another piece of fabric, although the edges of the top might be finished with a semblance of a border. Such quilt tops were often used as coverlets.

Redwork Friendship Quilt

Each of the blocks in this redwork friendship quilt is signed and dated, and located geographically. The blocks came from all over the United States, and the dates range from 1887 to 1896. The patterns come from a variety of sources.

Some magazines offered ink-stamping kits as premiums with each purchase, and women were encouraged to stamp blocks in the privacy of their own homes for sale to quiltmakers. The kits contained various inks, some washable, some not. Some of the inks had to be set with a hot iron. The women creating the pattern blocks used a sawtooth wheel with carbon paper to trace the lines. Later development of a sewing machine perforation attachment made the tracing process easier. Washable and permanent pens were also used to transfer patterns for quilt blocks.

Harper's Bazaar, The Ladies Home Journal, The Modern Priscilla, Peterson's, Godey's Lady's Book, Art Amateur, and *Butterick Needle Art* all competed for an embroiderer's money. Patterns of all shapes and sizes, using several different transfer methods, were available from many sources. Magazines, periodicals, ads, pattern companies, and catalogs of designs gave the customer a wide variety of choices. The unique combinations and derivations, as well as the composition of all these choices, make the results interesting. Magazines also offered premiums to entice the prospective customer.

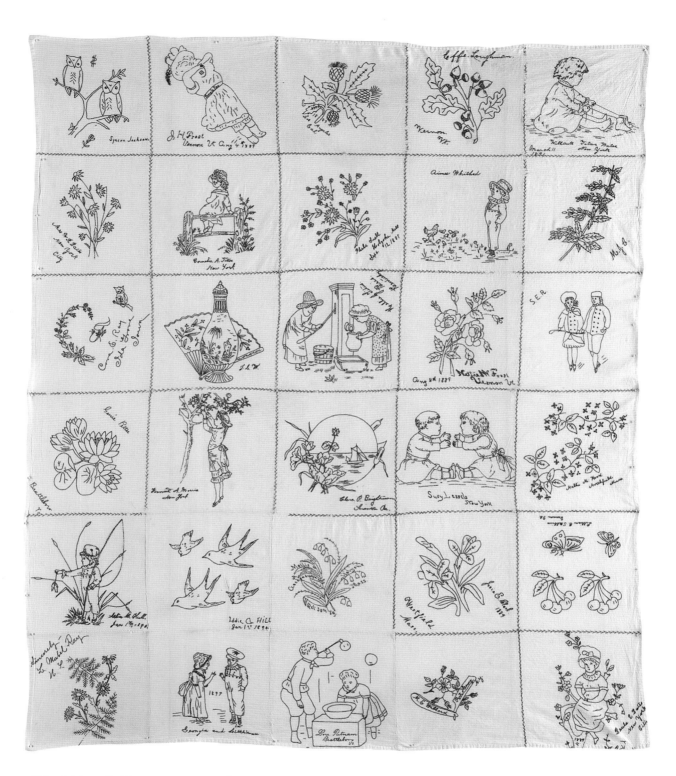

Friendship quilt | DATE: **1887–1891** | MAKER: **Various quiltmakers throughout the United States** | SIZE: **43" x 51"** | OWNER: **Annemarie Yohnk**

On this quilt, the edges of the top are brought to the back, where they are blind stitched. Feather stitching decorates the seams between the blocks.

Redwork Squares Placed on Point

Three generations worked on this redwork quilt, and there are initials on some of the blocks. The designs range from Botanicals to Penny Squares, and it was probably made between 1900 and 1920. Some of the patterns for this quilt could have come from the pages of the Home Beautiful catalog.

Mrs. T. G. Farnham of New York City started a business called Home Beautiful and issued a catalog of three thousand embroidery patterns in 1886. She originated or adapted a wide range of designs. Patterns were sold to be used in various ways. The same design, for example, might be used on a Crazy quilt or in a redwork quilt. In 1921, the Victorian Art Manufacturing Company of Cleveland, Ohio, began to produce only uniformly sized quilt block patterns, making it much easier for quiltmakers to create a quilt using pre-made patterns. Before this time, designs came in various sizes, and it could be difficult to find enough consistent in size for a quilt. The company stamped blocks in a rainbow of colors, perhaps to indicate the color of floss to be used. They offered kits with a stamped block of fabric, thread, needle, and instructions. The seams joining the blocks could be embellished with a feather stitch.

By 1930, stamped blocks, stamped tops, and kits could be purchased to make complete quilts, but few kits were for outline embroidery alone. Cross-stitch kits and appliqué kits with embroidery soon became available. Retail stores competed with magazines, and some stores even ventured into the mail-order business. Commemorative designs abounded, but those that were too elaborate were not as popular as simpler ones. Americans preferred practical patterns.

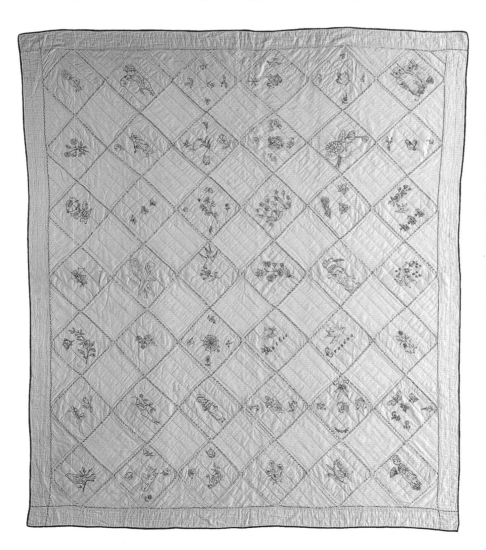

Redwork quilt | Date: c. 1900 | Makers: Adeline Crane, great-great-grandmother; Clara Cadwell, great-grandmother; Grace Grinnell, grandmother; Josephine Hellier, great-aunt | Size: 67" x 83" Owner: Rosemary Hoberg

Redwork quilt made in the early 1900s

Botanicals and Stars | DATE: c. 1910 | MAKER: **Mary Woehrmann**
OWNER: **Linda Wasmund** | SIZE: **72" x 83"**

Dark red stars accentuate the delicate embroidery designs in this redwork quilt.

REDWORK WITH EIGHT-POINTED STARS

Linda Wasmund found this quilt in her mother's house and has surmised that it was probably made by her maternal great-grandmother, Mary Woehrmann. Mary, who was born in Germany, emigrated to the United States as a young woman. She married, and she and her husband lived on a farm in Ohio, where they raised twelve children. The patterns are primarily Botanicals.

MOTHER GOOSE REDWORK QUILT

Mother Goose nursery rhymes, including Little Boy Blue, Three Blind Mice, Little Red Riding Hood, Little Jack Horner, and Jack and Jill, etc., are depicted on this redwork top. Nancy Clark lived in Connecticut when she made it. After she died, the family gave the quilt to her daughter, Mickey Loegering. Mickey lived in Minnesota, but she decided to sell the piece when she moved to Texas.

The children and animals featured in Mother Goose nursery rhymes and the fictional characters brought to life by artists such as Thorton Burgess (Peter Rabbit), Ruby McKim (Quaddy Quiltie Series), Kate Greenaway, and Bertha Corbett were popular sources for redwork quilt patterns. Popular culture also provided inspiration for new redwork patterns. The Japanese pavilion at the 1876 Exhibition in Philadelphia and *The Mikado*, the light opera by Gilbert and Sullivan, popular between the years 1884 and 1890, introduced the asymetrical concept of Japanese design. After the 1893 Chicago World's Fair, where a Christopher Columbus coverlet was on exhibit, designs of famous men and women from history began to appear.

Mother Goose nursery rhymes quilt | DATE: c. 1920 | MAKER: Nancy Clark | SIZE: 57" x 65" | OWNER: Annemarie Yohnk

Popular characters, such as those prominent in Mother Goose rhymes, were often the subject of redwork quilts.

The term "penny squares" was coined for designs featured at the Pan American Exposition in 1901.

RUBY MCKIM REDWORK QUILT

Designs from Ruby McKim's Quaddy Quiltie Series were used for this top. These patterns were created especially for redwork. McKim was a well-known quilter and designer, perhaps better known for her book containing 101 pieced quilt patterns than for the redwork designs used for this top. A close-up of the center of the top is shown here. In the design, the hunter sits in the middle square looking at the animals in the other squares. The quilter embroidered the pattern on feed sacks.

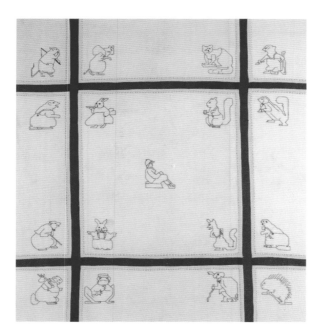

Quaddy Quiltie | DATE: c. 1916 | MAKER: Unknown SIZE: 85" x 89" | OWNER: Kathe Lemmerman

Quaddy Quiltie characters define the corners of this quilt.

Cross-Stitch Kit Quilts

The advances in technology associated with the red-work craze led to the cross-stitch embroidered quilt in the 1920s and 1930s. The designs were created using a single embroidery stitch—the cross stitch. Quite a number of these quilts surfaced during the Quilt Discovery Days. More cross-stitch quilts were found in southern Minnesota than in any other part of the state.

The use of the cross stitch to create a design went one step further than redwork. It was still basically a simple way to portray a pattern, but the design had to be abstracted into squares, each of which was filled with an X. The pattern companies that had been producing kits for the earlier embroidery products now began selling full-size cross-stitch quilt kits.

In the twentieth century, the need for young girls to learn needlework was diminishing. They no longer learned the alphabet by making samplers and were now going to school and exploring many subjects. But there was still the desire to create, and quilt kits provided an avenue to satisfy these cravings without having to do the design work.

Cross-stitch quilts in the medallion style had much more visual impact than the redwork quilts, and the cross-stitch style held its own against the appliqué kit quilts that were produced at the same time. Stamped quilt blocks for repeated-block quilts were sold by the dozen, with prices varying according to the size of the piece of stamped fabric.

Medallion Cross-Stitch Quilt

Pearl Johnson turned a kit from Herrschner's into this lovely quilt. The pattern and postage cost $8.20 in the company's 1954 mail-order catalog. Pearl learned quilting from her mother, Jonethe Sydnes, who also helped with the quilting of this piece. She has made twenty-eight quilts in a variety of styles.

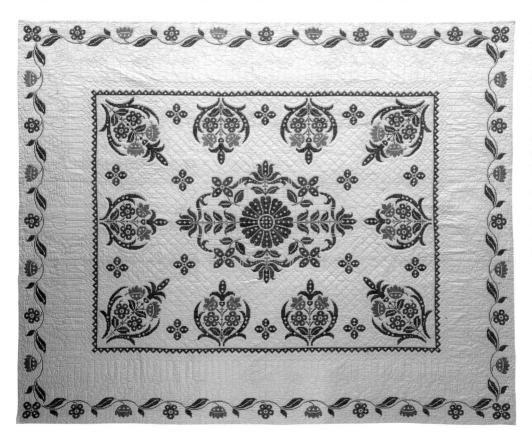

Central Flower Medallion
DATE: 1954
MAKER: **Pearl Johnson**
QUILTER: **Jonethe Sydnes**
SIZE: 80" x 95" | OWNER: **Pearl Johnson**

Cross-stitch quilts had more visual impact than the redwork quilts.

Cross-stitch quilt | DATE: 1974 | MAKER: Leona Burmeister | SIZE: 78" x 94" | OWNER: Dennis and Sylvia Burmeister

This cross-stitch quilt was a wedding gift for the maker's son.

ROSE CROSS-STITCH QUILT

The family of Sylvia Burmeister completed a number of quilts. This cross-stitched medallion, made by Leona Burmeister, was a wedding gift to her son Dennis and his wife Sylvia in 1974. Leona, her twin sister, Viola Breibarth, and their mother, Anna Breibarth, completed other quilts that are still in the family.

ROSE MEDALLION QUILTS

Flowers were often the inspiration for quilt designs. Here are two versions of a Rose Medallion. The similarity between the two patterns is striking, although one is more controlled while the other is lighter and less severe.

Gertrude Johnson made this version of a Rose Medallion in 1971. She created a quilt for each of her daughters, while this one went to her daughter-in-law, Dorothy Johnson. Gertrude did not start quilting un-

til she was in her forties, but she finished at least six quilts. She was seventy-five years old when she purchased this kit from Herrschner's catalog. Her quilting frame was set up in the dining room, and her sisters and sister-in-law often joined her there to work on the current project. Gertrude always said she could never get the dishes done fast enough so she could get back to the quilting frame.

The pattern of the second quilt is quite similar to Gertrude Johnson's quilt, but the execution is more controlled. Wanda Espeset found a quilt pattern for a Rose Medallion in a farm magazine and accepted her mother-in-law's offer to make Wanda a quilt. Cora Espeset finished this quilt in 1964, when she was seventy-five years old. Wanda used the quilt with a pink dust ruffle and plain pink and green quilted pillows to complete the ensemble. She intends to pass the quilt on to a granddaughter.

Rose Medallion | DATE: 1971 | MAKER: Gertrude Johnson | SIZE: 78" x 92" | OWNER: Dorothy Johnson

Lighter colors create a delicate Rose Medallion quilt.

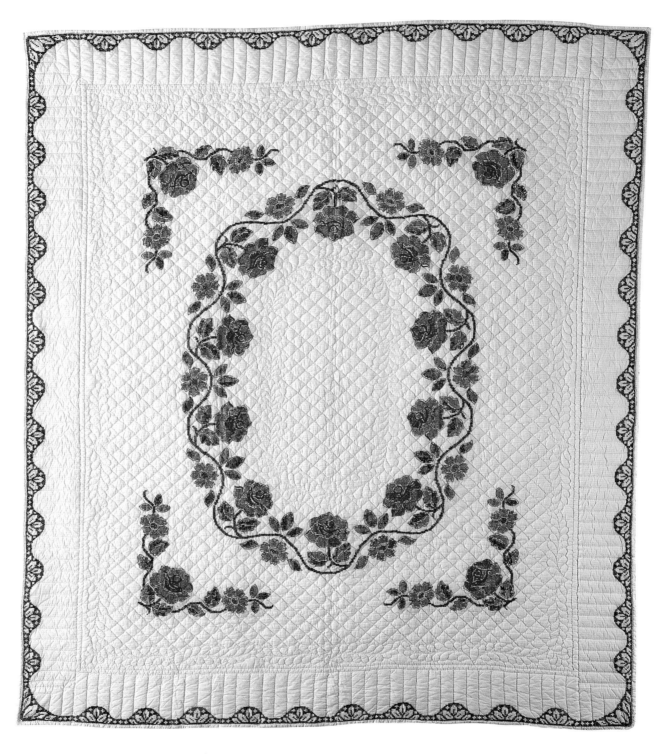

Rose Medallion | Date: **1964** | Maker: **Cora Espeset** | Size: **74" x 87"**
Owner: **Wanda Espeset**

Bold colors define this Rose Medallion.

Evening Star | **Date: 1941** | **Maker: Barbara Schroer** | **Size: 80" x 94"**
Owner: Kym Andrews

Dark-blue appliquéd snowflakes jump from this quilt's white background.

Snowflake cross-stitch | **DATE: 1960** | **MAKER: Lilly Eckstrom, quilted by Mamie Jonson** | **SIZE: 80" x 97"** | **OWNER: La Donna Levik**

Cross stitching gives the snowflakes on this quilt a delicate feel.

SNOWFLAKE CROSS-STITCH QUILTS

The companies supplying the designs for cross-stitch quilts did not hesitate to use variations on a theme. These two Snowflake-like patterns were akin to the Snowflake appliqué kit quilt of the same vintage. Again, one version is more controlled while the other, required much more embroidery, but has a lighter feeling. The contrasting border gives the one example a more dominating appearance. The Paragon kit, which cost $6.95 in 1941, was called Evening Star. Barbara Schroer, a self-taught quilter who began quilting when she was twenty-seven, made the quilt. It was one of eight quilts she finished.

In 1959, LaDonna Levik purchased the kit for this Snowflake quilt at Brett's Department Store in Mankato. LaDonna's mother, Lilly Eckstrom, embroidered the top and her grandmother, Mamie Jonson, quilted it. They began the quilt in January 1960 and finished by April of that same year. Lilly made more than twenty quilts. This one is a family heirloom, and LaDonna will pass it on to the next generation.

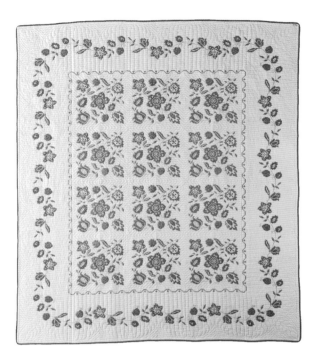

Repeated Block cross-stitch | Date: 1969 | Maker: Ida Christiansen, quilted by Lilian Giesler | Size: 80" x 93" | Owner: Irene Timm

A sharp, red edge defines this attractive cross-stitch quilt.

Repeated Block Pattern Cross-stitch Quilt
The repeated block pattern in this cross-stitch quilt is fanciful and not as regimented as many such quilts. Even the border has a free-form feel to it. Maker Ida Knutson, born in 1893, grew up on a farm in Otter Tail County. Her formal education ended at grade five, but she learned needle arts from her mother. In the early 1900s, land in northern Minnesota became available for homesteading. In 1914, Ida and her father filed claims for adjoining eighty-acre parcels. Ida was just twenty-one, and she had to live on the land for six weeks of the year to prove her claim. Her father and brothers built a ten-foot-by-twelve-foot log house with one window and one door. Ida married Christen Christiansen in 1915, and he acquired eighty acres next to her parcel.

They lived in the log house until they were able to clear more land, establish a garden, and build a barn for the horse and cow they had received as gifts. They worked hard and raised three children, two of whom graduated from the University of Minnesota. Christen built the school his children attended and was instru-

mental in getting electricity to rural areas and building grain elevators nearby.

Ida bought a used Singer treadle sewing machine for fifteen dollars and made clothes and bed linens from feed and flour sacks. She made quilts from the scraps. All three of her children have pieces of her work. Ida was seventy-six years old in 1969 when she made this red cross-stitch quilt. Her daughter, Lillian Giesler, quilted it. There are many hours of stitching, love, and history in the quilt that will live on when it is given to a granddaughter.

Twentieth Century Appliqué Kit Quilts

Kit quilts were created in response to the colonial revival home decorating movement of the 1920s. Women wanted to return to the crafts that were practiced during the colonial era. One of these was quilting, and kits were an easy way to begin to do this. A kit was supposed to contain everything necessary to make the quilt, but this was not always true. Sometimes extra fabric or other items, such as binding, would be needed to complete the project. Most kits were for appliqué quilts, although some pieced quilt kits or precut kits were available in a handful of designs.

Despite all the new technology, quilters were nostalgic for a simpler time. The manufacturers played on this dichotomy of emotions to market their wares. The names of kits echoed the established folk standard. The companies evoked the concept of the helpful relative who worked for the company. Aunt Martha, Grandma Dexter, or Aunt Dinah, could offer to help a quilter through the rough spots. Kit quilts were a legitimate way for a beginner to learn, and if she persevered and finished the quilt, she could be confident of a nice-looking product. Many quilters began with kits, and they rarely deviated from the published design.

Floral appliqué kits seemed to be designed by trained artists, but for the most part, the artists' names are unknown and determining the artists' identities is often difficult. Also, various museums have allowed companies such as Paragon and Bucilla to reproduce the designs from antique quilts in their collections,

**Four-Block appliqué kit | DATE: c. 1920
MAKER: Unknown
SIZE: 77" x 92"
OWNER: Private
Collection**

*Detailed quilting adds
texture to this appliqué
quilt.*

making it difficult to determine if a particular design is an original from the 1930s.

FOUR-BLOCK APPLIQUÉ KIT QUILT

The diversity of quilting patterns that accompanied the appliqué kits was varied and complementary. In many of the floral appliqué kits, the edges of the quilts are scalloped, a graceful finishing touch that added to the appeal of the kit. For a beginner this was not the easiest way to finish the border, but people bought the kits nonetheless. Kits typically cost less than buying all the materials necessary to make a quilt, and the tedious part of marking the components was already done, making kits irresistible during a time when there were few quilting manuals and classes available. Un-

like today, quilt guilds, experienced quilters, teachers, and books were few and far between, especially in rural areas, making it difficult for the individual to get started.

The companies selling these kits, including Bucilla, Progress, and Paragon, did, in effect, determine quilting trends. Mass-marketed kits created, guided, and molded the scope and direction of a quilter's proficiencies. As the arbiters of style, quilt kit companies set national rather than regional standards for performance. They overrode regional pattern names and established national names that sounded traditional. Names such as Windblown Tulips, Pansies, and Sunflowers were comforting and inspired confidence.

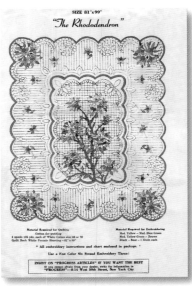

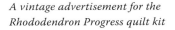

A vintage advertisement for the Rhododendron Progress quilt kit

Dogwood | DATE: 1956 | MAKER: Lea MacDonald | SIZE: 74" x 91" OWNER: Private collection

Dogwood blossoms grace this appealing kit quilt, completed with a yellow background.

Buyers were seduced by visual and emotional appeals and promises that the beginner had the necessary needlework skills to complete her own quilt. Judging from the number of unfinished kits that have surfaced, many buyers found the task of making the quilt to be more work than they had anticipated.

It is difficult to date the kit patterns, even if you have copies of catalogs from some of the kit manufacturers. Numbers were not always chronological or consistent for the same design. Bucilla was in business the longest, with Progress and Paragon not far behind.

APPLIQUÉ QUILT KIT

The background in the floral appliqué kit quilts was not always white or off-white. Lea MacDonald completed this appliquéd and embroidered Dogwood kit for her mother's birthday. She learned how to quilt from her grandmother, Myrtle Freshley, who has a quilt featured in another part of this book. Lea was a school teacher and home economist, and her husband was a professor of plant pathology at the University of Minnesota.

POPPY MEDALLION QUILT

There are numerous versions of poppy designs among the appliqué kits, including anything from Repeated Block to Four-Block to Medallion layouts. This lovely Poppy Medallion was made by Grace Osborne. Other quilts she has made have survived and are with various family members. Grace lived on a farm near LeCenter, Minnesota. She and her husband, Mike, raised eight children.

Poppy Medallion appliqué | Date: 1939 | Maker: **Grace Osborne** | Size: 80" x 92" | Owner: **Mary Jo Kaisersatt**

The quilting on this quilt is exceptional.

Tulip Appliqué
DATE: 1950
MAKER: Pearl Johnson, quilted by Agnes Wyborny
SIZE: 76" x 91"
OWNER: Charlene Kandt

Pastel tulips are the centerpiece of this appliqué quilt.

TULIP APPLIQUÉ KIT QUILT

In 1952, there was not the prejudice against kit quilts that was prevalent when the current quilt revival began in the late 1960s and early 1970s. Negative attitudes toward kit quilts are beginning to dissipate now that kits are again readily available. When Pearl Johnson made this quilt and entered it in the Minnesota State Fair in 1952, she won a blue ribbon. She completed this Tulip Appliqué kit from Herrschner's mail order catalog in 1950. It is one of more than two dozen quilts she made.

ROSE APPLIQUÉ QUILT

Marie DeLisle, a homemaker and milliner, purchased her kit for this Rose Appliqué quilt from Dayton's, a family-owned store in downtown Minneapolis, in 1955. (The Dayton name is synonymous with much that happened in the business and cultural affairs of the city at the time.) Large roses surround an intricate quilting pattern in the center, and rose buds are appliquéd in the borders. A scalloped edge completes the piece.

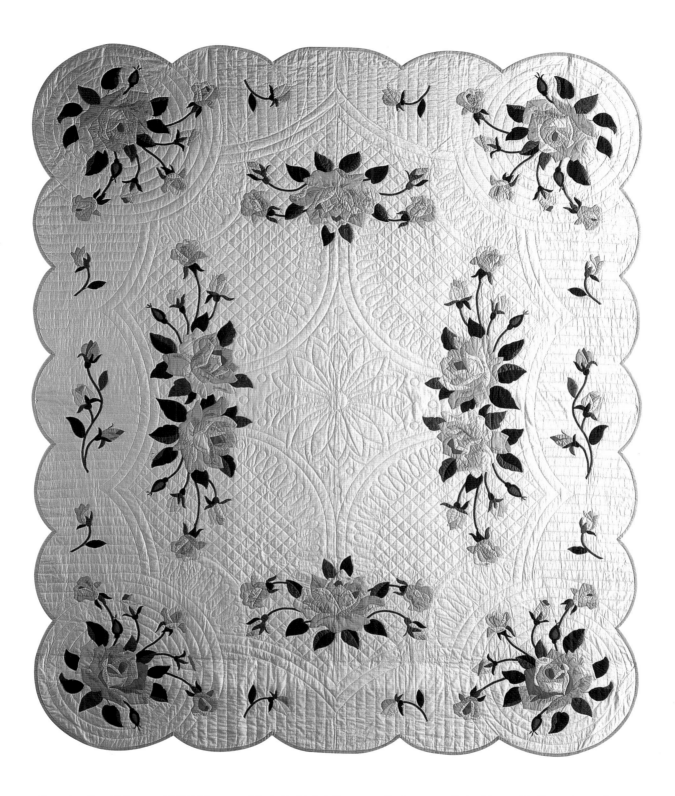

Rose Appliqué | Date: **1955** | Maker: **Marie DeLisle** | Owner: **Ruth Dietz** | Size: **76" x 92"**

Embroidery adds dimension to the appliqué roses in this 1955 quilt.

YELLOW ROSES QUILT

Eda Higgins was very particular and would not let anyone else work on her Yellow Roses quilt, as she said their stitches would not match hers. This kit was a combination of a Medallion and a Repeated-Block layout. The border is made of repeats of a block-size pattern. This was one of only two appliqué quilts Eda made, and her granddaughter, Betty Lewis, was the recipient.

Yellow Roses Medallion | **DATE:** c. 1930 | **MAKER:** Eda Higgins | **SIZE:** 78" x 90" | **OWNER:** Betty Lewis

A simple yellow rose is the basis for this medallion quilt.

Autumn Leaves | DATE: 1948 | MAKER: Estella E. Nelson | SIZE: 78" x 92"
OWNER: Betty Chesney

Leaves are both appliquéd and quilted on this crisp Autumn Leaves quilt.

AUTUMN LEAVES QUILT

In 1948, Estella E. Nelson purchased the kit for this Autumn Leaves Medallion quilt from Lee Wards, a craft store, and proceded to make the quilt. The quilting enhances the design and forms a herringbone grid in most of the background. The finished product was a gift for her daughter. Estella was born in up-state New York, but after getting married she lived in Cloquet and Duluth, Minnesota. Although she was trained as a nurse, Estella ran a trucking company after her marriage.

Yo-Yo Coverlets

Although not strictly quilts, as they have no batting or backing, Yo-Yo coverlets were popular from the 1920s through the 1940s. Most Yo-Yo coverlets were made from scraps, as circles of varying sizes could be easily cut from scraps of leftover fabric. The circles that make up a Yo-Yo coverlet are gathered around an edge that has been rolled over. The gathering stitch is then pulled tightly together until there is only a small opening. These gathered circles are tacked together to create the coverlet.

Where did the name originate? The wooden toy we associate with the name has a long history. As with quilting, the toy most likely originated in China. There are many examples of toys similar to the modern toy documented throughout history, but the word "yo-yo" comes from the Philippine version. This Filippino toy was introduced to the United States in the 1920s when Donald F. Duncan, Sr., purchased the Philip-

pine company that made yo-yos, advertised the toys widely, and sold many. The name yo-yo gained wide recognition at the same time the fabric version was becoming popular.

In the middle of the nineteenth century, dressmakers often used circles made from tape to create self-trims for garments as alternatives to expensive lace trims. In the 1870s, these decorative circles were made of fabric rather than tape. Called roses, the circles were sometimes added to appliqué quilts. In the December 1895 issue of *Peterson's Magazine,* Helen Burnside provided illustrated directions for making the fabric roses that would later be called Yo-Yos. The January 1888 issue of *Peterson's Magazine* featured an engraving of a "Marguerite Tidy"—gathered circles attached together with lacy stitches and the centers filled with yellow, worsted-yarn stitches to resemble daisies.

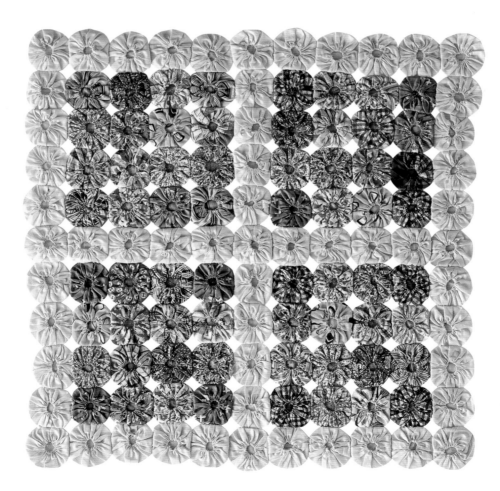

Yo-Yo | DATE: c. 1930 | MAKER: Unknown | SIZE: 24" square | OWNER: Private collection

A Yo-Yo pillow cover

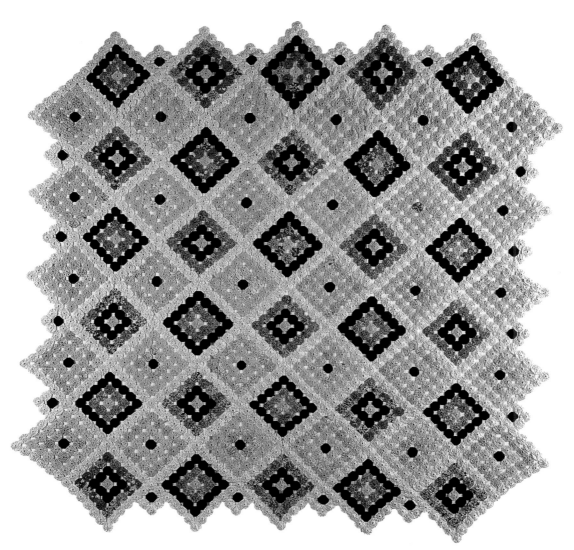

Yo-Yo | DATE: c. 1930 | MAKER: Unknown, found in southern Minnesota
SIZE: 76" square | OWNER: Private collection

Black, yellow, and white prints are the
predominant fabrics in this piece. It
is unusual to see a Yo-Yo coverlet as
visually striking as this one.

YO-YO PILLOW COVER

Yo-Yos were used for more than just coverlets. In the early twentieth century, the little circles were used to decorate small cosmetic bags and boudoir pillows or to embellish a quilt. Children's toys, such as clowns, were also created from columns of Yo-Yos, strung together to form the various parts of the body. Bells were sometimes added at the ends of the arms and legs.

YO-YO COVERLET

The Home Art Company of Chicago offered kits for "flower puff" pillows, quilt blocks, or quilts. "Puff" may come from the English name for the circles, Suffolk Puff, although the pattern also picked up the name

of "powder puff." These flower puffs were attached to muslin backgrounds to create coverlets. In the 1930s, the Yo-Yo technique was sometimes referred to as as a colonial heirloom pattern. The W. L. M. Company, of St. Louis, Missouri, used the designation "colonial heirloom" for one of its patterns—a Yo-Yo, Puff, or Bed of Roses quilt—in 1932.

After a while, the catchy name of Yo-Yo prevailed and the other names were forgotten. The popularity of the wooden Yo-Yo toy and the Yo-Yo name for the gathered fabric circles occurred at approximately the same time in the 1920s and 1930s. It is not too great a leap in logic to see the connection between the two.

Dresden Plate Quilts

The exact origin of the name for this quilt pattern remains unknown. Porcelain was made in Dresden, Germany, but no plate design produced there matches the plate pattern in a typical Dresden Plate quilt. Around the turn of the twentieth century, however, European and American women attending carnivals and dances did wear embossed flower-shaped decorations or cotillion orders that looked very much like the quilt pattern. These decorations, called Dresdens, were often used as Christmas ornaments as well. The Dresden Plate quilt pattern, then, could have taken its name from the shape of Dresden decorations and the china made in Germany.

Besides the Dresden Plate, there were a number of quilt patterns inspired by kitchenware: Broken Dishes, Bottles, Pickle Dish, Cake Stand, Cut Glass Dish, Ice Cream Bowl, Sugar Dish, Coffee Cups, Orange Squeezer, Bowl of Fruit, and so on. The Dresden Plate design was issued by no fewer than ten pattern publishers from the 1930s to the 1950s, which may account for its popularity. Mountain Mist (Stearns & Foster), *The Kansas City Star*, the Home Art Company, and *Suc-*

cessful Farmer all used the name Dresden Plate for the design. Nancy Cabot, the *Chicago Tribune's* quilt editor, called it Old Staffordshire after a type of china. Coats and Clark used the name Friendship Ring, and the *Oklahoma Farmer and Stockman* designated it Friendship Quilt.

There were many design variations, but all had a center circle, whether it was the background showing through or an applied one, with petals numbering anywhere from eight to twenty-four. The center circles were various sizes, and the petals could have round or pointed tops in multiple combinations. Pointed versions of the design sometimes included a small diamond between the points to form a second row to the design. Quilts featuring two sizes of the pattern were sometimes called Plates and Saucers. The Dresden Plate design looks very flowerlike and has also been called Aster, China Aster, Sunflower, Texas Sunflower, and even Pinwheel.

Creative renditions had novel sets of the blocks, varying the sizes of the motif, or they might have an unusual color scheme or background fabric. The cen-

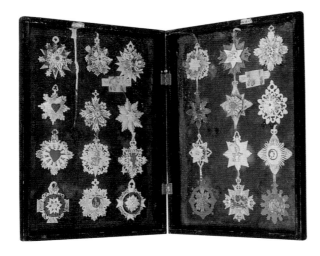

Above: Picture of collection of Dresdens from Early American Living *(Photograph © Bryson Leidich).*

Dresden Plate | DATE: c. 1910 | MAKER: Clara Hendrickson | SIZE: 64" x 98" | OWNER: Joyce Maul

Silk neckties work perfectly in the Dresden Plate pattern.

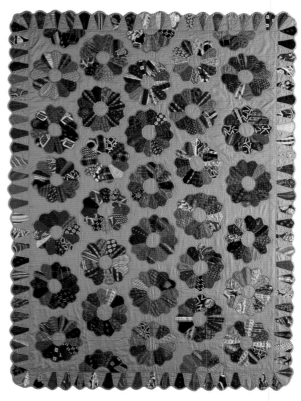

**Dresden Plate | DATE: 1941
MAKER: Johanna Klein | SIZE: 70"
x 85" | OWNER: Linda Pribyl**

*Bold blue zigzags separate the Dresden
Plates, giving this quilt a unique twist.*

tral medallion of a 1785 Anna Tuels quilt has a seg-
mented circular design around a center circle, which
may have influenced all the similar patterns to follow.
But the generally recognized Dresden Plate design is
thought to be of twentieth-century origin.

In some kits featuring repeated blocks, such as
the Dresden Plate, prints were used in sequence, or
perhaps the same print appeared in all its available
colors to give the appearance of a scrap quilt. Pre-cut
kits or ready-cut quilts were appreciated as there was
no wasted fabric. Quilters saved time and energy and
were assured a satisfactory product. Many Dresden
Plate quilts were documented in the state, but only
four examples, which illustrate a few of the placements
available to the quiltmaker, were selected to appear in
the book.

NECKTIE DRESDEN PLATE QUILT
Neckties were an easy source of fabric for Dresden
Plate quilts, as they were the ideal shape not only for

the plates themselves but also for the ice cream cone
border that quilters often used to finish the quilt. Clara
Hendrickson was born in Illinois but came to Minnesota at the age of twelve. When she made this quilt, she
decided to use a shiny fabric for the background to set
off the silk in the ties.

ZIGZAG DRESDEN PLATE QUILT
In this zigzag arrangement, Johanna Klein needed
only a minimum number of plates to complete her layout. In a Repeated-Block pattern arrangement, usually
twenty blocks were necessary. But the zigzag sashing
in this quilt filled the space that otherwise would have
required blocks.

Johanna made this quilt in 1941 before her marriage in 1943 at the age of nineteen. Johanna's nine
children kept her busy, interrupting her quiltmaking
until they had all married and left home. In later years,
the quilt frame was usually set up in the living room
for her enjoyment and that of her quilting friends.

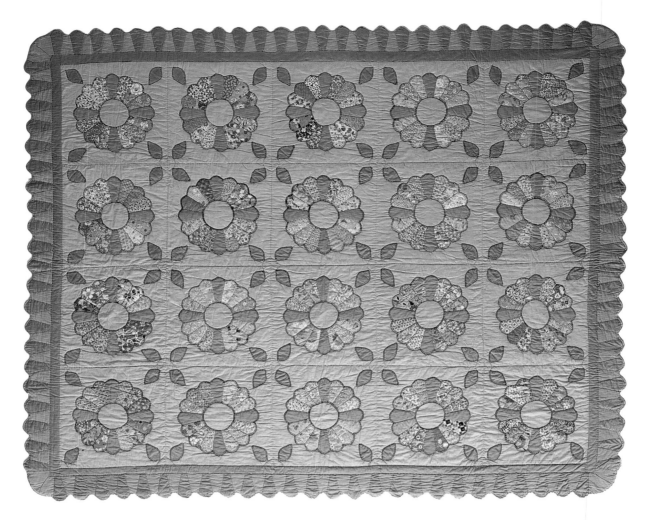

Dresden Plate | D A T E : c. 1950 | M A K E R : **Bergith Glaubitz, quilted by Bertha Brevig** | S I Z E : **69" x 84"** | O W N E R : **Nancy Swanson**

Yellow, green, and pink combine to create this appealing quilt.

DRESDEN PLATE QUILT

Bergith Glaubitz, her sister, Agnes Hagen, and her sister-in-law, Bertha Brevig, made between seven and ten quilts each year. The owner of this quilt, Bergith's grandniece, Nancy Swanson, remembers playing in the living room near where the frame stood and listening to the conversation as the ladies stitched. Many of the quilts were used until they were worn out. This one survived because Nancy's grandmother, Agnes Hagen, stored it in the attic.

As in Johanna Klein's quilt, there is embroidery around the center circle of the plate and the petals. Embroidery often embellished Dresden Plate designs, defining the center circle and outer edge of each petal. Buttonhole stitches in black embroidery floss commonly outlined the plates, but other colors were also used.

DRESDEN STAR QUILT

With the addition of triangles to the plate, this quilt was named Dresden Star, although one source called it the Kansas Sunflower. The border consists of triangles and the typical cone shape of the Dresden Plate pattern. When in her seventies, Ellen Lerdahl asked for scraps of fabric and old clothes from the family in order to piece quilts for family members. Within three months, she had completed four quilt tops. Her sister-in-law, Inga Samuelson, collected the tops to begin quilting. Apparently this top was not completely finished, as Inga had to use two different pieces of orange to complete it. The top was made during World War II, and fabric was hard to find. Ruth Herbst inherited the quilt when her mother, Inga, died.

Dresden Star | **DATE: c. 1930** | **MAKER: Ellen Lerdahl, quilted by Inga Samuelson** | **SIZE: 70" x 84"** | **OWNER: Ruth Herbst**

Quiltmaker Ellen Lerdahl made this Dresden Plate quilt with old clothing scraps.

Twentieth-Century Appliqué

In addition to the large companies that sold patterns, there were small cottage industries that contributed to the wide variety of patterns available. Marie Webster was the twentieth century's first trendsetting quilt designer. In her fifties, she was inspired by the Art Nouveau style, and she began to design patterns. Using pastel colors in her floral themes, her approach was a breath of fresh air. In January 1911, three of her quilts were published in *The Ladies Home Journal*, the first of fourteen quilts she designed that would be featured in less than two years.

There were so many requests for patterns for the designs that Marie soon found herself in the mail-order business. Family members and friends helped her produce and package the patterns. Her book, *Quilts: Their Story and How to Make Them*, the first book about American quilting, was published in 1915. Marie became a celebrity, giving lectures and writing articles, as she continued to create designs. Besides packaging patterns, her company, The Practical Patchwork Company, sold stamped tops, basted tops, and complete quilts. The company remained in the business through the 1930s.

The Stearns and Foster Company of Cincinnati, Ohio, became a potent force in the promotion of quilting in 1928 when it decided to change the packaging of

Marie Webster's Poppy | DATE: **1910–1920** | MAKER: **Unknown** | SIZE: **75" x 96"** | OWNER: **Private collection**

Marie Webster's Poppy pattern is a good example of a popular design. A red double border frames the center of this Poppy medallion.

SUNFLOWER APPLIQUÉ QUILT

Olive Fox found this Sunflower pattern on a Stearns and Foster batting wrapper and made this quilt sometime in the late 1930s or early 1940s. The handappliquéd and handquilted piece was one of approximately fifty quilts that Olive made in her lifetime. All of her quilts were handmade, and they often won blue ribbons at the Otter Tail County Fair. Her daughter-in-law, Stella Fox, is the proud owner of this quilt. Inspired by the beautiful quilts she inherited, Stella has become a quilter herself.

BUTTERFLY APPLIQUÉ QUILT

Butterflies, diamonds, and hexagons were some of the shapes commonly found in precut kits, and there is a good chance this is a paradigm. It is very well color coordinated with charming embroidered accents. The butterflies are placed on the diagonal within the squares, giving the impression they are flying. Susan Riley purchased this quilt at an antique show at the Minneapolis Convention Center.

Stearns and Foster Sunflower | DATE: c. 1930
MAKER: **Olive Fox** | SIZE: **84" x 88"** | OWNER: **Stella Fox**

The Sunflower quilt pictured here was created by Stearns and Foster designer Marie Webster.

its cotton batting to include patterns on the inside of the wrappers. Stearns and Foster also advertised and sponsored quilt exhibits to promote the sale of the batting, but the patterns on the wrappers were the most effective marketing tool.

Margaret Hays, an artist from Tennessee, was one of the pattern designers. She drew the pattern sheets, and Frederick Hooker, who thought of the name "Mountain Mist," designed the outside of the wrapper. The two worked together to write clear instructions for making the quilts. Phoebe Edwards took over when Margaret's contract ended, creating *The Mountain Mist Blue Book of Quilts*. A number of the patterns are duplicates of those used to make antique quilts.

Some are adaptations of the creations of others, as in the Sunflower quilt featured here. Marie Webster also drew a Sunflower quilt design which preceded this one. The aggressive marketing of Stearns and Foster and their claim that they were keeping classic quilting ideas alive had a profound effect on quilting in the 1930s.

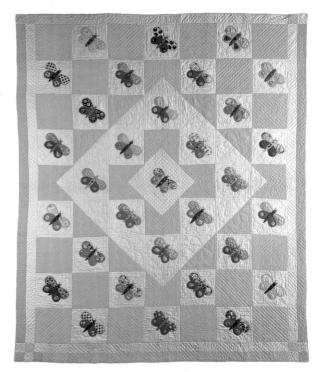

Butterfly | DATE: c. 1930 | MAKER: **Unknown** | SIZE: **73" x 89"** | OWNER: **Susan Riley**

Embroidery defines each of the appliqué butterflies on this quilt.

Rose of Sharon variation | DATE: 1900 | MAKER: Daisymae Allen | SIZE: 72" x 74" | OWNER: Paul and Beverly Allen

The style of this Rose of Sharon quilt echoes the Arts and Crafts designs popular at the time.

ROSE OF SHARON APPLIQUÉ QUILT

This very intriguing appliqué quilt was made around 1900 by Daisymae Allen, the grandmother of the present owner. The design seems to be a variation of the Rose of Sharon pattern. The Allen family is descended from relatives who came over on the Mayflower and has, after many generations, settled in Rochester, Minnesota.

LADY SLIPPER APPLIQUÉ QUILT

The women of the Wahpeton Tribe of Dakotas made this appliqué quilt. In 1972, it was presented on behalf of the state of Minnesota to Mary Christine Anderson, the state's first lady at the time. The Dayton Company organized the donation. The lady slipper, Minnesota's state flower, appears in both realistic and abstract forms on this machine-appliquéd and handquilted quilt. The piece is now part of the Minnesota Historical Society's collection.

Lady Slipper | D ATE: 1972 | M AKER: **Wahpeton Tribe of Dakotas** | S IZE: **93" x 106"** | O WNER: **Minnesota Historical Society**

Silk gives this quilt a rich, shimmering quality. (Courtesy of the Minnesota Historical Society)

Twentieth-Century Pieced Quilts

Anne Orr was a quilt artist known for her pieced quilts based on cross-stitch designs. In reality this trademark represented only about 15 percent of her total quilt designs. Anne's success as a designer was unrivaled, and a good number of her quilt kits were sold through *Good Housekeeping* magazine. It was said she received 500,000 requests for her brochure on one day in 1917. A pathfinder for women looking for professional opportunities in practical art, she ran the Anne Orr Studio of Nashville, Tennessee, while serving as the art/needlework editor of *Good Housekeeping* magazine. She wrote more than seventy books and pamphlets and judged several contests over the years. Her impact on the world of quilting was significant.

A NNE O RR Q UILT

Margaret Traxler, who owns this example of an Anne Orr design, was instrumental in organizing a quilt exhibit in Le Center, Minnesota. The exhibit remained up for a week and almost six hundred people came to view the quilts. As a result of Margaret's efforts, the town was later the site of a Quilt Discovery Day. Margaret purchased this quilt from the estate of Lydia Papke, who probably made it. The thousands of individual pieced squares in the top create the feel of a cross-stitch pattern. The medium values of rose and green give it a distinct identity.

There were many other types of pieced quilts that were popular in the twentieth century. Pictured here are a few examples found during the Quilt Discovery Days.

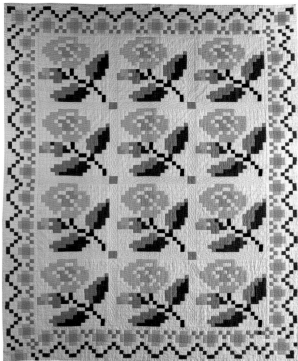

Roses | D ATE: **c. 1920** | M AKER: **Lydia Papke** | S IZE: **80" x 99"** | O WNER: **Margaret Traxler**

A quilted chain border defines each of the blocks in this quilt.

Trip Around the World | DATE: 1937–1938 | MAKER: Irene Anderson | SIZE: 83" x 88" | OWNER: Tom and Barbara Morstad

The bright colors of this quilt made for a cheerful wedding gift.

Laverne Morstad and her mother, Irene Anderson, with the quilt Irene made for Laverne's wedding.

Trip Around the World, Sunshine and Shadow | DATE: **c. 1930** | MAKER: **Anna Frenzen** | SIZE: **81" x 92"** | OWNER: **Edna Nelson**

A mint condition Trip Around the World quilt

TRIP AROUND THE WORLD WEDDING QUILT

Trip Around The World quilts were very common during the 1930s. Irene Anderson made this one for her daughter Laverne's wedding. Irene took her earnings from her first job and bought fabric at Norby's Department Store in Fergus Falls, Minnesota. She finished the top and delivered it to the nearby Wigdahl farm, where neighbors helped her quilt it. The batting came from pure carded wool of sheep belonging to Mrs. Wigdahl. When the ladies were not working on the quilt, the frame was raised to the ceiling.

SUNSHINE AND SHADOW QUILT

Maker Anna Frenzen called her Trip Around The World quilt "Sunshine and Shadow," because of the high contrast between the blues and the whites. Anna, of Clark, South Dakota, made the quilt in the late 1920s or early 1930s to give to her sister, Martha Nelson, of Wood Lake, Minnesota. When Martha died, the quilt was passed on to her daughter-in-law, Edna Nelson, of Echo, Minnesota. When documented, this quilt was in mint condition.

Fortune Wheel | DATE: **c. 1920** | MAKER: **Iva Spande** | SIZE: **76" x 90"**
OWNER: **Paul and Janice Spande**

A cone border frames this lovely pink and white quilt.

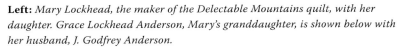

Left: *Mary Lockhead, the maker of the Delectable Mountains quilt, with her daughter. Grace Lockhead Anderson, Mary's granddaughter, is shown below with her husband, J. Godfrey Anderson.*

Delectable Mountains | DATE: 1924 | MAKER: Mary Lockhead | SIZE: 83" x 83" | OWNER: Grace Anderson

The triangles dominant in this quilt give the pattern its name.

FORTUNE WHEEL QUILT

Pink and white was a color combination much favored during the 1920s and 1930s when Iva Spande made this Fortune Wheel quilt. Iva had spread a newspaper, perhaps the *Minnesota Farmer*, on the bleachers to protect her dress while she was attending graduation exercises at the University of Minnesota. As she was picking up the newspaper, it fell open and she saw an ad for the Wheel of Fortune quilt pattern. She ordered it, prepared the stencils, and proceeded to make the quilt. The pattern and stencils are still among her sewing materials. Iva showed her future daughter-in-law, Janice, the quilt when she was dating Iva's son, Paul. It was love at first sight, and the quilt has since become a part of Paul and Janice's household. Iva made more than thirty quilts, but she was also a musician and teacher.

DELECTABLE MOUNTAINS QUILT

This version of Delectable Mountains, with its bright, contrasting pink and white color scheme, was made as a wedding quilt for Grace Lockhead when she married J. Godfrey Anderson in 1924. Grace was orphaned at thirteen and lived with her paternal grandparents in Sauk Centre, Minnesota. In 1989, Angeline Anderson, Grace's daughter-in-law, received the quilt as a keepsake, and it continues to be a family treasure. The quilt features a Delectable Mountain medallion center with a pieced rectangular inner border. It is handpieced with mitered corners in the border. The handquilting was done in a diagonal grid.

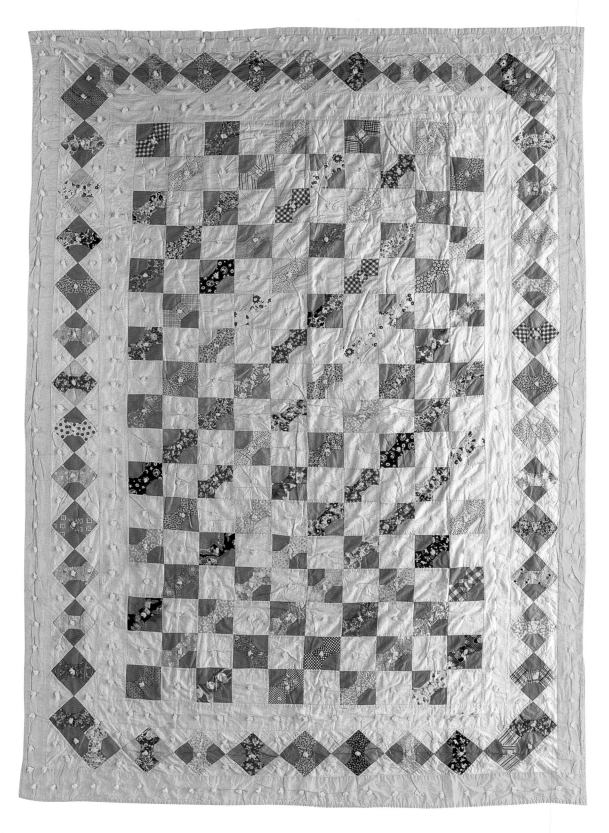

Bow Tie | DATE: **c. 1950** | MAKER: **Anna Martin** | SIZE: **62" x 90"**
OWNER: **Nancy Peterson**

The yellow yarn used to tie this quilt adds texture and dimension.

Blazing Star
DATE: 1937
MAKER: **Lyde McCollum**
SIZE: **74" x 88"**
OWNER: **Private collection**

The quilting on this yellow Blazing Star is exquisite.

TIED BOW TIE QUILT

Old clothes supplied the fabric for this Bow Tie quilt. The quilt was tied rather than quilted, and this forms part of its visual appeal. The blue background pieces create a nice contrast with the scraps used in the bow-ties. Maker Anna Martin was the oldest of thirteen children and had to leave school after the fourth grade because she was needed at home. Education meant a great deal to her, and she stressed to all of them the importance of finishing school as she had not been able to do so. She loved needlework and made gifts for all her grandchildren. Anna made other quilts in addition to this one between 1930 and 1950. She made this Bow Tie top around 1950 and her granddaughter, Nancy Peterson, finished it.

BLAZING STARS QUILT

Lyde McCollum of Minneapolis made this lovely multiple Blazing Star quilt in 1937. It was a commission from a neighbor who felt Lyde needed the money. The quilt was to be a gift for the neighbor's daughter. Lyde purchased all the yellow and white cotton sateen fabric at Amluxen's, a fabulous fabric store on Nicollet Avenue in downtown Minneapolis. After she finished the top, members of the Moravian Church in West Salem, Illinois, did the quilting. Unfortunately, the daughter for whom the quilt was made did not like yellow. The daughter faithfully took care of the quilt but never used it, eventually selling it to a private collector.

Endnotes

INTRODUCTION

1 Medalen, 1990 interview.

2 Millard, 1988 interview.

CHAPTER ONE

1 Krahn, Lisa, Sibley House Historic Site.

2 Barton, *John P. Williamson, A Brother to the Sioux,* 136.

3 Warner, Mary, Jan Warner, and Ann Marie Johnson. *Little Falls on the Big River,* 22–23.

4 Gilman, *Northern Lights,* 159.

5 "Duluth Woman 90 Years Old Has Interesting Relic of Geo. Washington," *Duluth News Tribune,* Oct. 7, 1907, 10.

6 Gilman, *Northern Lights,* 132.

7 "Women's Christian Temperance Movement." http://religiousmovements.lib.virginia.edu/nrms/wctu.html.

8 Aby, *The North Star State,* 391.

CHAPTER TWO

1 Adamson, *Calico and Chintz,* 14.

2 *Minnesota in the Civil War and Indian Wars.* (Last name misspelled as Busser; died in Galatin, Tenn. Jan. 28, 1865)

3 Stephens, October, 2003.

4 For more information on this designer, see Patterson, *Marion Cheever Whiteside Newton.*

5 Thieman, Nov. 15, 2003.

6 "Bridal Quilt." *Ladies Home Journal,* February 1940, 124.

7 Mielke, 2003.

8 Sitter, 2004.

9 Brackman, *Encyclopedia of Pieced Quilt Patterns,* 258.

10 Bodenhamer, June, 2003.

11 "Mora Woman Takes 91 Years in Stride." *Minneapolis Tribune,* Feb. 4, 1951.

12 *Needlecraft—The Home Arts Magazine,* February 1940, 124.

13 Plaines and Sears, 1994.

14 ibid.

15 ibid.

16 Bode, October, 2003.

17 Ramsey and Waldvogel, *Southern Quilts,* 132.

18 MacDowell and Fitzgerald, *Michigan Quilts,* 19.

19 Orlofsky, *Quilts In America,* 180.

20 Valentine, *West Virginia Quilts and Quiltmakers,* 33.

21 *The Janesville Gazette,* Obituary. April 18, 1888.

22 Carruth and Sinema, "Emma M. Andres and Her Six Grand Old Characters."

23 Peto, *Historic Quilts,* Chapter entitled "Quilts Designed and Made by Men."

24 Medin, October, 2003.

CHAPTER THREE

1 Brackman, *Clues in the Calico,* 118–119.

2 Kaplan and Ziebarth, *Making Minnesota Territory 1849–1858,* 31–37.

3 Brackman, *Signature Quilts,* 25–37.

4 Brackman, *Encyclopedia of Pieced Quilt Patterns,* 420–421.

5 Kauthold, 2003 interview.

6 Helping Hands Quilters meeting minutes, 1966–1967.

7 Starnes, *The Paynesville Press,* September 12, 1984.

8 Clark, Ronsheim, and Knepper, *Quilts in Community,* 107.

9 Vollmer, interview.

10 Brackman, *Encyclopedia of Pieced Quilt Patterns,* 214–215.

11 Minnesota Historical Society, 1864 Horton quilt research papers.

12 Clark, Ronsheim, and Knepper, *Quilts in Community,* 108.

13 Khin, *Collector's Dictionary of Quilt Names and Patterns,* 211.

14 Brackman, *Encyclopedia of Pieced Quilt Patterns,* 54.

15 Schoenborn, August 1988 interview.

16 Schoenborn, August 1988 interview.

17 Khin, *The Collector's Dictionary of Quilt Names and Patterns,* 372

18 Marling, *Blue Ribbon,* 17–26.

19 Third Annual Fair of the Minnesota Agricultural Society Premium Book, Minnesota Historical Society Collection.

20 Marling, *Blue Ribbon,* 20–21.

21 Birdsall, "Designs are Myriad..." *Saint Paul Pioneer Press,* August 24, 1952.

22 Minnesota Historical Society Collection, Fifth Annual Fair of the Minnesota State Agricultural Society Premium Book.

23 Birdsall, "Designs are Myriad..." *Saint Paul Pioneer Press,* August 24, 1952.

CHAPTER FOUR

1 Ferrero, *Hearts and Hands,* 73.

2 Waldvogel, *Soft Covers for Hard Times,* 40.

3 Ferrero, *Hearts and Hands,* 74.

4 Kohter, *Forget Me Not,* 107.

5 Calculations of the Federal Reserve Bank based on the year 1913, the earliest year available in their Consumer Price Index and Inflation Rate conversion chart.

6 Orlofsky, *Quilts in America,* 98.

8 Connolly, "Recycling Feed Sacks and Flour Bags," *Dress,* 1–36.

CHAPTER FIVE

1 *Godey's Lady's Book,* April 1850, 285.

2 Abbott, October 2003.

3 Brackman, "A Chronological Index to Pieced Quilt Patterns 1775 to 1825." *Uncoverings 1983* 4.

4 Gunn, "Victorian Silk Template Patchwork in American Periodicals 1850–1875," *Uncoverings 1983* 4.

5 Green, 2003.

6 Detert, 1990.

7 Root, 2003.

8 Brackman, "A Chronological Index to Pieced Quilt Patterns 1775 to 1825." *Uncoverings 1983* 4.

9 Orlofsky, *Quilts in America,* 209.

Tribute to Joyce Aufderheide

(1920–1991)

Joyce Aufderheide, pictured here with the quilt she loaned to Joan Mondale to be hung in the vice president's office while Walter Mondale was the incumbent.

In Minnesota, Joyce Aufderheide, played an important role in keeping the tradition of quilting alive during the quiescent years between 1940 and 1970. Joyce collected many quilts. Her quilt museum in New Ulm, Minnesota, was called Hands All Around and operated from 1969 to 1985. She hosted several public exhibits of the majority of her collection in various venues in New Ulm. The provenance was known on many of the quilts in Joyce's collection because she was able to acquire them from the original maker's families. Some of the quilts are signed or initialled and dated. Examples range from 1790 to the 1970s, and most are in excellent condition.

In the 1950s, Joyce was far ahead of her time. As she gave talks on the subject of quilting around the country, she stressed that during the 1950s quilting seemed to be one of the few acceptable outlets for women to express their creativity and opinions. She lectured nationally for more than twenty years and was a noted quilt historian and appraiser. She was often quoted and mentioned in quilt publications.

Visitors came to New Ulm from more than twenty countries and all fifty states to view her quilt collection. In 1977, Joyce loaned one of her quilts to Walter Mondale's wife, Joan, to be hung in the vice president's office while he was the incumbent. Other quilts from her collection were exhibited at the Minneapolis Institute of Arts.

Joyce fostered quiltmaking in her area as well as in the Midwest and throughout the country. She also designed quilts, including the Brown County Bicentennial quilt. She was a very special person, and her death in 1991 was a great loss to Minnesota quilters and to the whole quilting world.

Bibliography

Abbott, Carolyn. Letter to Minnesota Quilt Project, October 2003.

Aby, Anne ed. *The North Star State: A Minnesota History Reader.* St. Paul: Minnesota Historical Society Press, 2003.

Adamson, Jeremy. *Calico and Chintz: Antique Quilts from the Collection of Patricia S. Smith.* Meridan, Conn.: Hull Printing, 1997.

Barton, Winifred. *John P. Williamson, A Brother to the Sioux.* Minnesota: Sunnycrest Publishing, 1980.

Birdsall, Amy. "Designs are Myriad – Quilts Catch Eye At Fair." *Saint Paul Pioneer Press,* August 24, 1952.

Brackman, Barbara. *Clues in the Calico: A Guide to Identifying and Dating Antiques Quilts.* McLean, Va.: EPM Publications, 1989.

_____. *Encyclopedia of Appliqué.* McLean, Va.: EPM Publications, 1993.

_____. *Encyclopedia of Pieced Quilt Patterns.* Paducah, Ky.: American Quilter's Society. 1993.

_____. "Signature Quilts: Nineteenth-Century Trends." *Uncoverings 1989* 10. Research Papers of the American Quilt Study Group.

_____. "A Chronological Index to Pieced Quilt Patterns 1775 to 1825." *Uncoverings 1983* 4.

Bode, Lois. Letter to Minnesota Quilt Project, October, 2003.

Bodenhamer, Faye. Letter to Minnesota Quilt Project, June, 2003.

Breneman. Judy Anne Johnson. "Friendship Quilts: Precious Remembrance." Womenfolk Web site. http://www.womenfolk.com/quilting_history/friendship.htm.

_____. "From Redwork to a Rainbow of Colors." Womenfolk Web site. http://www.womenfolk.com/historyof quilts/midcentury.htm.

_____. "Quilting, Alive Beneath the Surface." Womenfolk Web site. http://www.womenfolk.com/historyof quilts/midcentury.htm.

Brick, Cindy. "The Kate Greenaway Story." *The Quilting Quarterly,* Summer 2001.

"Bridal Quilt." *Ladies Home Journal,* February 1940, 124.

Bullar, Lacy Folmar, and Betty Jo Shiell. *Chintz Quilts: Unfading Glory.* Tallahassee, Fla.: Serendipity Publishers, 1983.

Bunchuck, Kim. "The History of the Sunbonnet Sue Quilt Pattern." Web site of Kim Bunchuck, quilter, mother, fabric collector. http://www.sunbonnetsue.com/suehistory.html.

Carruth, Janet, and Laurene Sinema. "Emma Andres and Her Six Grand Old Characters." *Uncoverings 1990* 11: 88–108.

Cerny, Catherine A. "Quilt Ownership and Sentimental Attachments: The Structure of Memory." *Uncoverings 1997* 18: 95–119.

Clark, Ricky, Ellice Ronsheim, and George Knepper. *Quilts in Community: Ohio Traditions.* Nashville, Tenn: Rutledge Hill Press, 1991.

Connolly, Loris. "Recycling Feed Sacks and Flour Bags: Thrifty Housewives or Marketing Success Story." *Dress: The Journal of the Costume Society of America.* 19 (1992): 1–36.

Cook, Anna Lue. *Textile Bags (The Feeding and Clothing of America).* Florence, Ala.: Books Americana, 1990.

Copeland, Anne, and Beverly Dunvient. "Kit Quilts in Perspective." *Uncoverings 1994* 15: 144–167.

Cord, Xenia E. "Signature Quilts." *Blanket Statements,* no. 74 (Fall 2003). Newsletter of the American Quilt Study Group.

_____. "Marketing Quilt Kits in the 1920's and 1930's." *Uncoverings 1995* 16: 39–174.

Cowles, Julia Darrow. "The Mother of the Sunbonnet Babies." *Stitch 'n Sew Quilts Magazine,* March/April 1988. Reprinted from *Housekeeper,* September 1907.

Crews, Patricia Cox, and Ronald Naugle. *Nebraska Quilts & Quiltmakers.* Lincoln: University of Nebraska Press, 1991.

Curious Works Press and the Charleston Museum. *Mosaic Quilts: Paper Template Piecing in the South Carolina Lowcountry.* Charleston, SC: Curious Works Press and the Charleston Museum, 2002.

Detert, Zelda. Interview, 1990.

Eanes, Ellen, et al. *North Carolina Quilts.* Chapel Hill: University of North Carolina Press, 1988.

Early American Living, Christmas 1999: 59. Magazine of historic homes.

Federal Reserve Bank of Minneapolis Web site. "What is a Dollar Worth?" http://woodrow.mpls.frb.fed.us/Research/data/us/calc.

Ferrero, Pat. *Hearts and Hands.* San Francisco: The Quilt Digest Press, 1987.

Filo, Jill Sutton. "Ruby Short McKim, The Formative Years." *Uncoverings 1996* 17: 63–94.

Finley, Ruth E. *Old Patchwork Quilts And The Women Who Make Them.* McLean, Va.: EPM Publications, 1992.

Furgason, Mary Jane, and Patricia Cox Crews. "Prizes from the Plains: Nebraska State Fair Award-Winning Quilts and Quiltmakers," *Uncoverings 1993* 14: 188–217.

Gilman, Rhoda R. *Northern Lights: The Story of Minnesota's Past.* St. Paul: Minnesota Historical Society Press, 1989.

_____. *The Story of Minnesota's Past.* St. Paul: Minnesota Historical Society Press, 2003.

Godey's Lady's Book, April 1850.

Graubard, Stephen ed. *Minnesota, Real & Imagined: Essays on the State and Its Culture.* St. Paul: Minnesota Historical Society Press, 2000.

Green, Ruth. Letter to Minnesota Quilt Project, 2003.

Grover, Eulalie Osgood. *Sunbonnet Babies Primer.* Chicago: Rand McNalley and Company, 1902.

Gunn, Virginia. "Victorian Silk Template Patchwork in American Periodicals 1850-1875," *Uncoverings 1983* 4.

_____. "Yo-Yo or Bed of Roses Quilts: Nineteenth Century Origins." *Uncoverings 1987* 8: 129–146.

Hagerman, Betty. *A Meeting of the Sunbonnet Children.* Baldwin City, Kan.: self-published, 1979.

Harding, Deborah, *Red & White: American Redwork Quilts and Patterns.* New York: Rizzoli International Publications, 1992.

Hedges, Elaine. *Hearts and Hands: Women, Quilts, and American Society.* Nashville, Tenn.: Rutledge Hill Press, 1987.

Helping Hands Quilters meeting minutes, 1966–1967.

Hinson, Delores. *The Sunbonnet Family of Quilt Patterns*. Upper Saddle River, NJ: Prentice Hall Press, 1983

Home Arts Needlecraft Magazine, February 1949.

Houck, Carter. *The Quilt Encyclopedia Illustrated.* New York: Harry N. Abrams, 1991.

Johnson, Mary Elizabeth. "Quilter's Notebook." *Country Living,* October 1996.

Kaplan, Anne R., and Marilyn Ziebarth, eds. *Making Minnesota Territory: 1849–1858.* St. Paul: Minnesota Historical Society Press, 1999.

Kauthold, Bernadette, interview, October 2003.

Khin, Yvonne. *The Collector's Dictionary of Quilt Names and Patterns.* Washington, D.C.: Acropolis Books, 1980.

Kiracofe, Roderick, and Mary Elizabeth Johnson. *The American Quilt: A History of Cloth and Comfort 1750-1950.* New York: Clarkson Potter, 1993.

Kohter, Jane Bentley. *Forget Me Not: A Gallery of Friendship and Album Quilts.* Pittstown, Va.: Mainstreet Press, 1985.

Kort, Ellen. *Wisconsin Quilts: Stories in the Stitches.* Charlottesville, Va.: Howell Press, 2001.

Krahn, Lisa, Sibley House Historic Site.

Lass, William E. *Minnesota—A History.* New York: W.W. Norton & Company, 1977.

Lipsett, Linda Otto. *Remember Me: Women and Their Friendship Quilts.* San Francisco, Calif.: The Quilt Digest Press, 1985.

MacDowell, Marsha, and Ruth D. Fitzgerald. *Michigan Quilts: 150 Years of a Textile Tradition.* East Lansing: Michigan State University Museum, 1987.

"Marie Webster." *McCalls Quilting* (Vintage Quilts issue), Spring 2001.

Marling, Karal Ann. *Blue Ribbon: A Social and Pictorial History of the Minnesota State Fair.* St. Paul: Minnesota Historical Society Press, 1990.

Medalen, Janet, Interview, May 25, 1990.

Medin, Leona. Letter to Minnesota Quilt Project, October, 2003.

Mielke, Marlene. Letter to Minnesota Quilt Project, 2003.

Millard, Arlene. Interview, May 20, 1988.

Miller, Susan Price. "Carlie Sexton and Her Quilt Pattern Business." *Uncoverings 1996* 17: 29–62.

"Mora Woman Takes 91 Years in Stride, Keeps Busy Quilting and Knitting." *Minneapolis Tribune,* February 4, 1951.

Nelson, Rick. "Flour Power." *Minneapolis Star Tribune,* September 11, 2003.

Nicoll, Jessica. "Signature Quilts and the Quaker Community, 1840-1860." *Uncoverings 1986* 7: 27–37.

Oliver, Valerie. "History of the Yo-Yo." Spintastics Skill Toys Web site. http://www.spintastics.com/History of yo-yo.asp.

Orlofsky, Patsy, and Myron Orlofsky. *Quilts in America.* New York: McGraw-Hill, 1974.

Patterson, Naida Treadway. "Marion Cheever Whiteside Newton: Designer of Story Book Quilts, 1940–1965." *Uncoverings 1995* 16: 67–94.

Perry, Rosalind Webster, and Marty Frolli. *A Joy Forever: Marie Webster Quilt Patterns.* Santa Barbara, Calif.: Practical Patchwork, 1992.

Peto, Florence. *Historic Quilts.* New York: American Historical Company, 1939.

Plaines, Karen and Judy Sears. Oral interview with Hazel Roemhildt for Minnesota Quilt Project, 1994.

"Quilt Kits to Show and Tell," *Traditional Quiltworks,* no. 71: 5–6.

Ramsey, Bets, and Merikay Waldvogel. *Southern Quilts: Surviving Relics of The Civil War.* Nashville, Tenn.: Rutledge Hill Press, 1998.

Root, Jeannette. Letter to Minnesota Quilt Project, 2003.

Schoenborn, Martha. Interview, August 1988.

Sitter, Kathryn. Letter to Minnesota Quilt Project, 2004.

Stafford, Carleton L., and Robert Bishop. *American Quilts and Coverlets.* New York: Weathervane Books, 1974.

State of Minnesota Board of Commissioners. *Minnesota in the Civil War and Indian Wars.* St. Paul, Minn.: Pioneer Press, 1890.

Stephens, Ruth. Letter to Minnesota Quilt Project, October, 2003.

Stitch 'n Sew Quilts Magazine. March/April 1988.

Starnes, Barbara. "Quilters, following their predecessors' patterns, these "sew-ciable" women use needle and thread to earn money for charity." *The Paynesville Press Newspaper,* September 12, 1984.

"Sunbonnet Sue, A Bit of History"

Thieman, Phyllis. Letter to Minnesota Quilt Project, November 15, 2003.

Trestain, Eileen Jahnke. *Dating Fabrics: A Color Guide (1800–1960).* Paducah, Ky.: American Quilter's Society, 1998.

Upham, Warren. *Minnesota Place Names: A Geographical Encyclopedia.* St. Paul: Minnesota Historical Society Press, 2001.

Valentine, Fawn. *West Virginia Quilts and Quiltmakers: Echoes from the Hills.* Athens: Ohio University Press, 2000.

"Vintage Quilt Kits," *Traditional Quiltworks,* no. 63: 41–43.

Vollmer, Merle. Interview.

Waldvogel, Merikay. *Soft Covers for Hard Times: Quiltmaking and the Great Depression.* Nashville, Tenn.: Rutledge Hill Press, 1990.

———. "The Origins of Mountain Mist Patterns," *Uncoverings 1995* 16: 92–138.

Warner, Mary, Jan Warner, and Ann Marie Johnson. *Little Falls on the Big River: A History of Little Falls Minnesota for Kids.* Little Falls, Minn.: Morrison County Historical Society, 2001.

West St. Paul (MN) *Sun,* May 26, 1987, 1.

Wilens, Patricia, ed. *Mountain Mist Quilt Favorites, For the Love of Quilting.* Des Moines, Iowa: Oxmoor House, 1998.

Winter Park (Fla.) Public Library, History and Archives Collection. Eulalie Osgood Grover Collection. http://www.wppl.org/wphistory/EulalieGrover/.

"Women's Christian Temperance Movement." Religious Movements, University of Virginia Website. http://religiousmovements.lib.virginia.edu/nrms/wctu.html.

Index

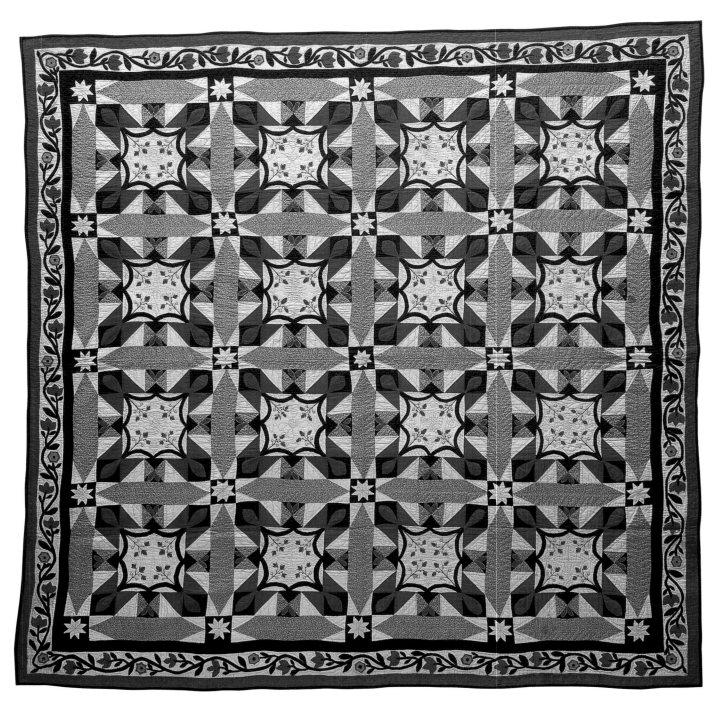

Tulip Quilt | DATE: c. 1870 | MAKER: Ann Summerville
Hodgins | SIZE: 86" x 86" | OWNER: Stevens County
Historical Society